Essential Histories

The Boer War 1899–1902

Essential Histories

The Boer War 1899–1902

Gregory Fremont-Barnes

First published in Great Britain in 2003 by Osprey Publishing,
Midland House, West Way, Botley, Oxford OX2 0PH, UK
443 Park Avenue South, New York, NY 10016, USA
Email: info@ospreypublishing.com

ISBN-13 : 978-1-84176-396-5

A CIP catalogue record for this book is available from the British
Library

Editor: Sally Rawlings
Design: Ken Vail Graphic Design, Cambridge, UK
Cartography by The Map Studio
Index by Alan Rutter
Picture research by Image Select International
Originated by PPS Grasmere Ltd., Leeds, UK
Typeset in Monotype Gill Sans and ITC Stone Serif
Printed in China through Bookbuilders

07 08 09 10   11 10 9 8 7 6 5 4

For a complete list of titles available from Osprey Publishing
please contact:

NORTH AMERICA
Osprey Direct, C/o Random House Distribution Center,
400 Hahn Road, Westminster, MD 21157
E-mail: info@ospreydirect.com

ALL OTHER REGIONS
Osprey Direct UK, P.O. Box 140,
Wellingborough, Northants, NN8 2FA, UK
E-mail: info@ospreydirect.co.uk
www.ospreypublishing.com

Contents

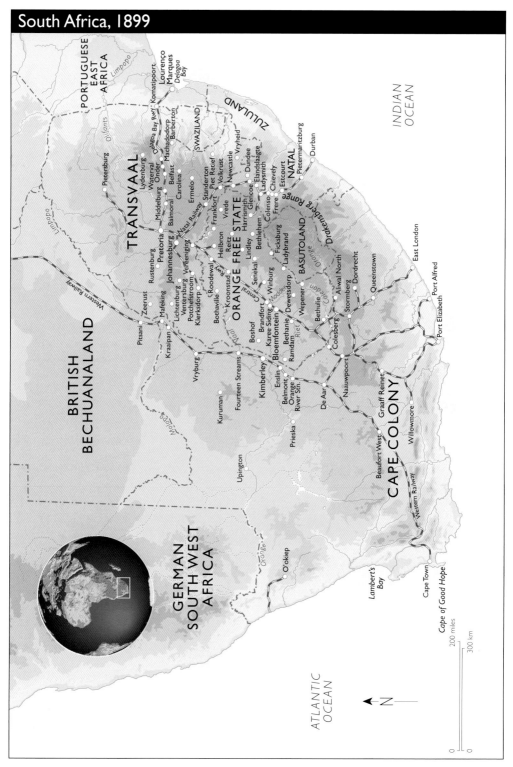

The total area of the four belligerent states was vast: 475,000 square miles, mostly consisting of high tableland, known as the High Veld, rising to about 4,500 feet above sea level. The wide, sometimes undulating, open spaces of the veld – mostly scrub, bush and boulders – provided ideal conditions for the highly mobile Boer forces. The small rocky hills, known as kopjes, provided them with useful points of observation and excellent defensive positions, especially when entrenched. October to March (spring and summer in the southern hemisphere) would be hot or very hot during the day and cold at night, with clear air offering long-range visibility. Dirt roads quickly turned to quagmires of mud in the frequent, sudden torrents of summer rain. In dry weather convoys and troop movements threw up clouds of dust in their wake.

Introduction

Addressing the House of Commons in May 1896, the British Colonial Secretary, Joseph Chamberlain, made a remarkable prediction about the nature of a future war with the Boers. He declared,

A war in South Africa would be one of the most serious wars that could possibly be waged. It would be in the nature of a civil war. It would be a long war, a bitter war, and a costly war ... It would leave behind it the embers of a strife which I believe generations would hardly be long enough to extinguish ...

Chamberlain's prediction was greeted with general skepticism, yet he was ultimately proven right. When hostilities began in October 1899, easy victory appeared a foregone conclusion to the many British observers who blithely announced that the war would be 'over by Christmas'. After all, the Boers appeared to possess nothing more formidable than a small amateur army composed of simple farmers, while Britain could deploy a highly trained professional force which had an unbroken record of success in its other imperial campaigns. The Boers, many of whom were themselves equally confident of victory, soon shattered such illusions. Indeed, the war gave the British Empire, in the words of Rudyard Kipling, 'no end of a lesson', and Britain eventually required no fewer than 450,000 men to subdue an enemy that was never stronger than 60,000 men at any one time. The struggle continued for nearly three years, from 1899 to 1902, producing heavy casualties on both sides and bringing suffering and misery to hundreds of thousands of Boer civilians, many of whom were to die in British custody.

The Boer War, generally referred to by contemporaries in Britain as the 'South African War', was unlike any other conflict of the Victorian era. Nearly all such campaigns had been waged against native armies whose bravery and motivation was no match for a well-equipped professional force. Britain had always been able to rely on its tactical sophistication and the quality of its training and weapons to counterbalance the numerical superiority of these indigenous tribesmen, however resolute and highly disciplined. The only other major conflict fought by Britain in this era had been the Crimean War (1854–56), a war fought against European troops, with both sides employing tactics, weapons and even uniforms largely unchanged since Waterloo, 40 years before. Indeed, the traditional scarlet coat of the British infantryman still remained the hallmark of the army three decades after the Crimea.

The Boer War was an entirely different affair. The Boers were armed with modern, smoke-free, repeating rifles, accurate at great distances. The individual marksman was seldom to be seen as he issued fire from cover. The days of lines of men with bayonets lowered for the charge, great massed columns, soldiers deployed shoulder to shoulder, and glaringly inaccurate smoothbore muskets, were at an end. The Boers were largely an unseen force, and confronting them with traditional volley fire or hand-to-hand fighting proved difficult, if not impossible.

In the Crimea, a gallant officer who waved his sword in the air while leading his men forward, bayonets at the ready, stood some chance of surviving the charge. To attempt such folly on a South African battlefield was to mark oneself out for certain death in a hail of rifle fire. British officers eventually adapted themselves to the new realities of war, replacing their swords with revolvers and stripping their uniforms of the insignia that betrayed their rank.

Boer civilians in a British concentration camp. Images of enfeebled, emaciated and dying children were not simply the product of anti-British propaganda, but a cruel reality for thousands of innocent victims. (Ann Ronan Picture Library)

Yet their troubles did not end there. Even if the Boers were driven off, suffering only minor losses, they simply remounted and rode away, ready to fight another day. Through superior mobility they consistently denied their opponents the opportunity even to face them in battle, much less to deliver a decisive blow. It was one thing to recognize that tactical changes would have to be made, it was quite

another to implement these changes. The British Army, having experienced decades of success in other campaigns, was a deeply conservative institution. Many in senior positions bluntly refused to accept that numerous reforms would be required were its professional forces to outfight these amateurs.

The Boer War straddled two centuries not only in its chronology, but in the very manner in which it was fought. At first the fighting bore many of the hallmarks of 19th century warfare. The conflict as a whole was later characterized by the celebrated military historian, J. F. C. Fuller, as 'The Last of the

Australian mounted troops. After 'Black Week' such men brought welcome benefits to the British war effort. Proficient in horsemanship and accustomed to intense heat and open country, Australians were also generally fitter and hardier than their British counterparts, many of whom were drawn from slums. (Ann Ronan Picture Library)

Gentlemen's Wars.' Both sides exercised a certain degree of chivalrous conduct, not least to the wounded. The fact that deaths from disease still exceeded those suffered in action also placed the war in a clear 19th century context.

Yet the Boer War also witnessed the introduction of elements of warfare that we would associate more with the 20th than the 19th century. Specifically, new forms of technology were employed, such as the field telephone, searchlights, barbed wire and the heliograph, a mirrored device using flashes of sunlight to send signals in Morse code over considerable distances. Tactics changed significantly in order to cope with entrenched adversaries armed with rifles and machine-guns. For example, infantry advances in open order under the protection of a creeping artillery barrage were introduced. The war highlighted the efficacy of guerrilla warfare. This in turn led to a number of ruthless responses, including the policy of 'scorched earth,' whereby British patrols roamed the

countryside, setting fire and laying waste to vast stretches of the veld. Most shocking of all, British military and civil authorities rounded up and interned tens of thousands of civilians in concentration camps. When the war ended, there were more civilian than military dead, an indication of the way in which the conflict shifted over time from conventional to guerrilla fighting.

To some, as Chamberlain intimated, it was virtually a civil war, pitting as it did at times Boer against Boer and, more generally, whites against whites, in marked contrast to Britain's many other colonial conflicts. Indeed, many British memoirs refer to 'Brother Boer'. Yet recent research reveals what black Africans already knew. It was not strictly a 'white man's war,' as it was popularly characterized at the time. From the start blacks were swept up into the conflict as laborers, scouts and spies for both sides, sometimes as combatants for the British, but mostly as innocent victims of a war fought by a race alien to their continent.

The unanticipated length of the conflict further distinguished the Boer War from other British colonial conflicts. It was also the first to inspire the interest of thousands of people back home. The general public, now enjoying a higher standard of literacy than ever before, benefited from novel rapid forms of communication that brought news even from a front thousands of miles away. For the first time, large numbers of people in Britain could and did follow the fortunes of their own soldiers at the front through newspapers, letters and postcards.

Dozens of war correspondents flocked to South Africa. The *Daily Mail* alone sold nearly a million copies every day in 1900, and 'Tommy Atkins,' as the ordinary British soldier was popularly known, could, unlike his predecessors in the Crimea, record his daily experiences and the events of the war for posterity. The period also saw the first cinematographic films. Many soldiers took the newly available portable camera to the front, bringing the sights of war home. It was also the first war in which substantial numbers of volunteers, from the working class all the way to the upper class, came forward to join the colors, making this the first 'people's war.' Indeed, the British Army, supported for the first time by volunteer troops from the Queen's self-governing 'white colonies' – Australia, New Zealand and Canada – grew to a size never previously conceived of by the Victorians.

All of these features represented the future of warfare. The 20th century had dawned. Queen Victoria (1819–1901), who had reigned for most of the 19th century, died before the war was over, and the conflict came to mark the end of an era. This was at once the last of the great colonial wars and the first modern conflict.

If the conduct and scale of the war in South Africa came as a sudden shock to British soldiers and civilians alike, its outbreak certainly did not. Rather, it came as the result of a long process of deteriorating relations between Britain and the Transvaal, with whom the other Boer republic, the Orange Free State, maintained a defensive alliance.

Many Boers believed that their republics had been divinely ordained and therefore would not give them up without a fight. The

Boers lived a simple, largely rural existence. They were a patriarchal, God-fearing people for whom the new conflict was but one of a series of actions fought in defense of their republics against an empire greedy for land and for the immensely lucrative natural resources of the region. First they had left the Cape in search of independence from alien rule; next they had lost Natal; then the British had annexed Transvaal, only to lose it again in their first serious military encounter with the Boers. Now the British wanted to wrest independence from innocent farmers by seizing two sovereign nations without provocation – a sort of heroic struggle waged by the Afrikaner 'volk' against the Goliath Britain. With their freedom under threat, nothing remained for the Boers but confrontation with the source of that menace, whatever the odds against them.

The British perspective was naturally rather different. Many saw the war as a defense of the rights of thousands of their countrymen living abroad, peacefully asserting their claims to political rights as long-term, tax-paying residents. By extension, imperialists believed that Afrikaner nationalism threatened British interests and security in South Africa in general, not least because it blocked the natural extension of British capitalism and empire-building on a continent to which all the great European powers were then frantically laying claim. In addition to strategic factors, economic considerations also played a part in the origins of the war. By the mid 1880s the deep gold mines of the Witwatersrand had proved the area to be one of vast wealth. The Transvaal was marked out as the new economic superpower of South Africa. Thrown into this explosive mix were such personalities as Joseph Chamberlain, Alfred Milner and Cecil Rhodes, all fervent imperialists.

In its most simplistic form, the struggle may be seen as one of aggressive British imperialism pitted against equally aggressive Boer nationalism: would Britons or Boers achieve mastery over South Africa?

Chronology

British defeat of 'Black Week'
18 December Lord Roberts replaces
Buller as Commander-in-Chief of
British forces in South Africa, with
Kitchener as Chief of Staff

1900   **6 January** Action at Platrand, outside
Ladysmith
10 January Roberts arrives at Cape
Town
23–24 January Battle of Spion Kop
5–7 February Battle of Vaalkrans
11 February Roberts opens his
campaign
14 February Fight for Tugela Heights
begins
15 February Relief of Kimberley; Boers
victorious at Waterval Drift
18 February Battle of Paardeberg
27 February Cronjé surrenders at
Paardeberg; British finally victorious at
Tugela Heights
28 February Relief of Ladysmith
March British begin erecting
blockhouses
7 March Action at Poplar Grove
10 March Battle of Driefontein
13 March British occupy
Bloemfontein unopposed
15 March Roberts offers amnesty to
Boers prepared to surrender their
weapons, the so-called 'hands-uppers'
17 March Boers adopt policy of
guerrilla tactics in tandem with
continued conventional resistance
31 March Action at Sannah's Post
3–4 April Action at Mostertshoek
5 April Action at Boshof
12 May Boer attempt to enter
Mafeking fails
17 May Relief of Mafeking
24 May Orange Free State annexed to
British dominions as Orange River
Colony
29 May Actions at Doornkop and at
Biddulphsberg
30 May Roberts enters Johannesburg
5 June Roberts occupies Pretoria
7 June De Wet strikes British supply
lines at Roodewal
12 June Action at Diamond Hill

16 June Roberts issues proclamation
on burning of farms
31 July Boers under Prinsloo capitulate
to the British in Brandwater Basin
27 August Action at Bergendal
October General ('Khaki') election in
Britain; 'pro-Boers' receive scant
support
19 October Kruger leaves South Africa
for Europe; Schalk Burger appointed
acting-president
25 October British annex the
Transvaal
6–7 November Action at Leliefontein
29 November Kitchener replaces
Roberts as Commander-in-Chief, who
leaves for England on 10 December
13 December Action at Nooitgedacht
16 December Kritzinger and Hertzog
invade Cape Colony
27 December Arrival of Emily
Hobhouse to visit concentration camps

1901   **28 January** In the Transvaal, French
begins massive drive to round up Boers
31 January Action at Modderfontein
10 February De Wet invades the Cape
28 February Abortive peace talks
open at Middelburg
16 May Kritzinger launches second
invasion of the Cape
28 May Action at Vlakfontein
July Committee under Millicent
Fawcett appointed to inspect
concentration camps
17 September Actions at Elands Poort
and Blood River Poort
30 September Action at Moedwil
11 December Kritzinger begins third
invasion of the Cape
25 December Action at Tweefontein

1902   **28 February** Extensive British drive
culminates with success at Lang Reit
7 March Action at Tweebosch
11 April Battle of Roodewal
6 May Action at Holkrantz
15–17, 29–31 May Peace conference
convened at Vereeniging
31 May Treaty of Vereeniging signed;
Boer forces surrender
June–July Boer prisoners of war released

Historical roots of the conflict

European settlement of southern Africa began in 1652 when the Dutch East India Company, in search of a provision station and port of call on the route to the East Indies, sent Jan Van Riebeeck to the Cape of Good Hope. Within a few years a farming community of settlers, 'burghers,' sprouted, supplying meat and vegetables to passing ships. By 1657 the Dutch fell out with the local native tribe and wrested grazing lands from them. Shortly thereafter the settlers moved into the interior, beyond the reach of the Dutch East India Company, and in doing so began a tradition of independent living which would become the hallmark of their descendants. But the burghers were not to be completely self-sufficient, for at the same time they brought slaves into their settlement. Shortly into the new century the burghers numbered about 1,800, including some Huguenots who had fled the persecutions of Louis XIV, and a thousand slaves. By the early 18th century these farmers, or Boers, had developed a dialect of Dutch which, over time, developed into Afrikaans, and a new race of people – Afrikaners – came into being. Some of them populated the area around Cape Town, but most lived in isolated farmsteads on the veld, living hard, frugal lives based on Dutch Calvinism and a fierce individualism. The land was, in their view, theirs by the grace of God, and they felt a natural superiority over the natives, with whom they frequently fought and whom they sometimes subjugated.

The Cape remained a Dutch colony until 1806 when a British expedition, seeking to dispossess Napoleon's ally of an important strategic post on the vital route to India, landed and seized the colony. The British formally annexed the Cape in 1815, and £6 million was given to Holland in compensation. Relations between the British authorities and the new wave of settlers, and the Boers, deteriorated with the abolition of

slavery within the British Empire in 1833, which the Boers bitterly resented. This interference in their way of life not only threatened them economically, but introduced an element of democracy inconsistent with the Boers' sense of their own racial superiority over black Africans.

Therefore, between 1836 and 1840 approximately 4,000 'Voortrekkers,' or early migrants, set out north on what became known as the 'Great Trek' in search of new lands to cultivate and freedom from British rule. Once across the Orange River the Boers divided between those settling in the Transvaal, and those who proceeded east into Natal. This second group, under Piet Retief, negotiated a treaty with the Zulus in February 1838, but Retief and his men were then treacherously massacred at a gathering ostensibly arranged to celebrate the agreement. Nearly 300 other Boers were also killed in a raid on their camp, prompting retaliation from those who remained. On 16 December the decisive battle of Blood River took place beside the Ncome, where 3,000 Zulus were killed out of a force of about 10,000 when they flung themselves against a wagon laager defended by a mere 530 Boers, of whom only three were wounded behind the tightly chained vehicles. Over succeeding decades there would be numerous other confrontations with indigenous peoples, but Blood River must be marked out as a seminal event in the development of Afrikaner identity. Thereafter, Afrikaners saw their victory as divinely given and the event led to the establishment of three communities – in the Transvaal, in the area that would become known as the Orange Free State, and in Natal.

It was not long, however, before British influence extended into the new areas settled by the Voortrekkers. Britain annexed Natal in 1842, cutting off the Boers' access to the sea by taking the strategic port of Durban. Nevertheless, by the Sand River Convention of 1852 Britain did recognize the sovereignty of the Transvaal (officially, the South African Republic or Zuid Afrika Republik (ZAR)), and two years later withdrew from the area north of the Orange River, which then became the Orange Free State. British interest in the region resumed with the chance discovery, in 1867, of diamonds. This discovery triggered a rush of several thousand prospectors to the area along the Orange, Vaal and Harts Rivers. But it was not until three years later that the discovery of diamonds in dry soil on a farm owned by Johannes Nicolaas de Beer caused the influx of tens of thousands of fortune-seekers and, in 1871, the mining town of Kimberley sprouted up with a population of 50,000 people, the focus of an extremely

lucrative industry. At about the same time Britain annexed Griqualand West, an area also rich in diamonds, despite the outcry caused in the Orange Free State.

By this time the Boers harbored great suspicions of British intentions in South Africa, which were by no means allayed when the British Foreign Secretary, Lord Carnarvon, proposed a federation of South African states. Self-rule was granted to the Cape Colony and £90,000 paid to the Free State as compensation for Griqualand West.

Diamond mining. The development of this industry around Kimberley quickly transformed what had been a largely agricultural economy into an urban center. Vast amounts of British capital investment flowed in to fund mineral extraction and the construction of railways. (Ann Ronan Picture Library)

Battle of Isandlwana, 22 January 1879. The conflict with the Zulus opened disastrously when a British force of 1,200 men was wiped out in the opening days of the war. By July, however, Zulu power was broken and their lands were soon incorporated into Natal. (Ann Ronan Picture Library)

Britain's intentions became all too clear when it annexed the Transvaal on 12 April 1877 amidst bitter protests from the inhabitants. This marked the end of Boer independence and was a severe blow to Afrikaner pride. Afrikaner nationalism flourished, not simply in the Transvaal itself, but in the Cape Colony as well. Still, no military resistance followed British annexation. True, many Afrikaners welcomed the comprehensive defeat of the Zulus by the British in 1879, but the threat posed by native Africans had been dealt with in the past. To the Boers, the British were not protectors, but occupiers.

Transvaalers soon adopted a policy of passive resistance. Twice they sent Paul Kruger (1825–1904) to London, where he was informed that the annexation would stand. Finally, in December 1880, the Transvaalers proclaimed their independence and took up arms in what became known as the 'First Boer War' or the 'Transvaal War.' The British commander in the area, Sir George Pomeroy Colley (1835–1881), suffered first a minor defeat at Laing's Nek, and then utter disaster at Majuba Hill on 27 February 1881, an occasion significant enough to the Boers to merit its adoption as a national holiday.

Back in London, the Liberal Government under Gladstone, not regarding the stakes as high enough to warrant a continuation of the conflict, concluded peace by the Pretoria Convention on 5 August. Britain did not completely restore Transvaal independence, but rather maintained that republic under her suzerainty, which in effect meant that Britain bore partial responsibility for the republic's foreign affairs and controlled domestic legislation pertaining to blacks. Further negotiations took place with the new government under Paul Kruger. A veteran of the Great Trek, he was something of an Old Testament-style patriarch who personified Boer nationalism. By the London Convention of 27 February 1884 the Transvaal was granted full internal independence, but the precise definition of British suzerainty was not even then absolutely specified. Several years later Britain added St Lucia Bay to Natal as a further means of ensuring that the Transvaal remained landlocked. That this was a

Battle of Majuba, 27 February 1881. The decisive action of the First Boer War. Major-General Sir George Colley, with 400 men, thought his elevated position a strong one, but Boer marksmanship and mobility led to Colley's death and a British rout. (Ann Ronan Picture Library)

deliberate policy there seems little doubt, for the British had already annexed Zululand, Bechuanaland (now Botswana), Basutoland, and other territories, blocking access to the sea.

All these events suggested to the Boers that, first, British forces were badly led and could be defeated with little effort. Secondly, the remarkably favorable peace offered by the Pretoria Convention, and confirmed later at the London Convention, suggested that the British preferred to avoid a heavy military commitment to South Africa, sought only limited political objectives in the region, and were reasonably satisfied with an independent Transvaal. Still, it seemed Britain wished to hem in the republic wherever possible.

Amidst the political wrangling, diamond mining carried on apace, soon shifting from the business of individual diggers to large-scale enterprises led by mining companies employing armies of white and black laborers, the blacks earning considerably less

than their white counterparts. Capitalist investment flowed in, not least from men already possessed of great wealth like Cecil Rhodes (1853–1902), who founded the De Beers Mining Company in 1880. Rhodes, an Englishman, possessed a keen business sense and an unswerving commitment to British imperialism. He said,

If there be a God, I think that what he would like me to do is to paint as much of Africa British-red as possible and to do what I can elsewhere to promote the unity and extend the influence of the English-speaking race.

British authorities in South Africa, in fact, needed no encouragement: a British commission headed by the Lieutenant-General of Natal was appointed to determine ownership of the land around Kimberley, with the result that the area was soon annexed and incorporated into the Cape Colony, of which Rhodes was shortly to become Prime Minister.

The region proved even more lucrative than originally believed. In 1886 gold was discovered on the Witwatersrand, in the southern Transvaal, about 65 km (40 miles) south of Pretoria. This immediately propelled

the Transvaal – largely agrarian and poor – into the ranks of the wealthiest countries in the world. A new city, Johannesburg, with the area around it, sprouted up as the richest gold-bearing region in the world, with

Paul Kruger, first president of the Transvaal. A strict Calvinist, he was the archetypal Boer image of a pastoral, God-fearing and fiercely-independent people convinced of their right to the land they had acquired earlier in the century. His suspicions of the threat posed by British imperialism were probably justified. (Ann Ronan Picture Library)

Cecil Rhodes, one of several personalities who played an important role in the breakdown of British–Boer relations. During the war Rhodes was trapped in Ladysmith. He offered abundant supplies of food and weapons, but was nearly arrested for his constant criticism of the commanding officer. (Ann Ronan Picture Library)

favorable mining concessions granted to foreigners. Eager to profit from this unexpected boom, and to reap fortunes just as businessmen and prospectors had in California in the 1850s, tens of thousands of foreign investors, miners and other settlers poured in from across the world. In the 10 years to 1896, Britons, Australians, Canadians, Germans and others, known to the Boers as Uitlanders ('outsiders'), together with rural Afrikaners and Africans, swelled the population of Johannesburg to 100,000.

Like the diamond industry, gold production became the business of major mining magnates like Alfred Beit and Julius Wernher, the so-called 'Randlords' who had millions of pounds to invest and large numbers of laborers eager for work. Labor costs were kept down to the bare minimum, the mostly unskilled African element of the labor force was paid a tiny fraction of what their white counterparts received, and were housed on site in squalid accommodation. Thus, the discovery of gold and diamonds brought profit on a massive scale, for the Witwatersrand accounted for one-fifth of the world's gold production and the area around Kimberley, mostly owned by Rhodes, was responsible for 90 percent of the world's diamond production by 1891. Rapid industrialization came to South Africa, imposing on a traditional, largely rural, conservative and religious society altogether new ideas brought in by the massive influx of foreigners. There had been fewer than 250,000 whites in South Africa in 1870. By 1891 this figure had rocketed to 600,000. Most of these had settled in the Transvaal, the very place where the Trekkboers had sought quiet isolation from Europeans and a pastoral life, earlier in the century.

This massive influx of, for the most part, British nationals introduced a significant new development in British–Boer relations. Possessing alien ideas on morality, religion, business practices and education, these economic immigrants brought in their wake a host of vices attendant on a rapidly growing economy: gambling, prostitution and violence. Worse still, the Uitlanders were thought to threaten not only the traditional moral and religious base of Afrikaner society, but the very political system of the Transvaal. The Uitlanders, if granted political rights, could by their very numbers have swamped the Afrikaner population and refashioned society completely through the extension of the vote. This could, for instance, have led to some form of limited franchise for blacks, which already existed in the Cape Colony, an idea that was unthinkable to the Boers. To prevent this, in 1890 the Volksraad, the Transvaal parliament, increased the period of residence required for the right to vote and the acquisition of citizenship from five to 14 years. Most of the Uitlanders had no interest in losing their British citizenship, but a minority, particularly some of the prominent mine owners, were beginning to demand the right to participate in Transvaal political affairs.

As immigrants began to flood in, Kruger also viewed with dismay what appeared to be the encirclement of his country. The British annexed Zululand in 1887, creating further barriers to the Transvaal's access to the sea. Everywhere else the pressure from British territory seemed to be growing: the Cape Colony to the south and south-west, Natal and Zululand to the east, and Bechuanaland to the north-west. There were now sound reasons for believing the very existence of the Transvaal was at stake. The British had

annexed the Transvaal before: now they could do so again, on the pretext of protecting the interests of the substantial British expatriate community. Moreover, in the neighboring British possessions of Cape Colony and Natal, wealthy capitalists and industrialists had come to wield considerable political power. Kruger had good reason to fear that they would attempt to extend their influence into the Transvaal.

Imperialism – a guiding principle of the age – also played a part in the origins of the war. Men like Rhodes were enthusiastic proponents:

I contend that we are the finest race in the world, and that the more of the world we inhabit, the better it is for the human race. Just fancy, those parts that are at present inhabited by the most despicable specimens of human beings, what an alteration there would be if they were brought under Anglo-Saxon influence.

Such views found strong support in Britain. Success in the 'Scramble for Africa,' in which Britain, France, Germany and Belgium had been involved since the 1870s, depended on expanding one's own possessions while impairing the growth of those of other nations. Germany, which had annexed a sizable portion of south-west Africa, was a particular concern. Rhodes hoped to play his part in expanding British imperial territories by eventually linking Cairo to Cape Town by one continuous railway. This would only be possible if Britain controlled the Transvaal and the Orange Free State, which he foresaw joined together in a federation of South African colonies. Through his South Africa Company, established by Royal Charter in 1889, Rhodes already exercised considerable control over Matabeleland (called Rhodesia from 1895) to the north of the Transvaal, which he had seized in 1893. As Prime Minister of the Cape Colony he made concessions and deals with Afrikaners whom he believed might be prepared to cooperate in some future South African federation under British control.

Rhodes also had a personal stake in the fall of the Transvaal Government, for he and other leading industrialists already objected to the high rate of taxes on such vital mining commodities as dynamite, and

Joseph Chamberlain, secretary of state for the colonies. Like Sir Alfred Milner and Cecil Rhodes, one of the key figures responsible for pushing Britain and the Boer republics toward war in order to open the way for their annexation as imperial dominions. (Ann Ronan Picture Library)

controls on access to the railways on which the industry depended. Thus, in Rhodes's mind, Kruger represented an obstacle not only to the growth of the British Empire in South Africa, but also a bar to the expansion of the Randlords' own business empires based on gold and diamonds.

By the middle of the 1890s the Transvaal found itself flanked by British territory on its western, northern and south-eastern sides, with Delagoa Bay in Portuguese East Africa

Jameson and his raiders at Doornkop, 2 January 1896. Bound for Johannesburg, where they hoped to support an uprising that in fact never materialized, they were stopped short, surrounded by a Boer force and forced to surrender after token resistance. (Ann Ronan Picture Library)

(now Mozambique) the last conduit through which the Boer republic could maintain trade and communication abroad without British interference. The Portuguese consistently refused to sell the port to Rhodes, and in 1894 the Transvaalers secured access to the coast – and therefore economic independence from British possessions – with the completion of the railway line between Pretoria and Delagoa Bay.

Meanwhile, relations with Britain continued to decline with the election of the Unionist (Conservative) Party in June 1895. The new government under Lord Salisbury (1830–1903), in particular the Colonial Secretary, Joseph Chamberlain (1836–1914), naturally had close links with Rhodes in his capacity as Prime Minister of the Cape Colony. Many Boers drew the conclusion that the British wanted nothing less than complete control over the region.

Such conclusions were well founded. Events then took a dramatic turn as a result of an intervention by Rhodes. Utterly foiled in his attempts to isolate the Transvaal before bringing it under the British flag, Rhodes plotted with prominent Uitlanders to seize power by force, on the pretext that Uitlanders were discontented on political and economic grounds. The so-called Reform Committee was to foment an uprising in

Johannesburg, while Dr Leander Starr Jameson (1853–1917), a protégé and friend of Rhodes, was to ride to the Uitlanders' assistance from Bechuanaland with several hundred mounted paramilitary volunteers and topple the Transvaal Government. The conspiracy had the covert backing of Joseph Chamberlain; Rhodes expected it to succeed and intended the British High Commissioner in the Cape, Sir Hercules Robinson, to mediate a settlement which would bring the Transvaal under British administration.

Jameson's ill-conceived raid in fact came to an ignominious end at Doornkop on 2 January 1896. A strong Boer force led by General Piet Cronjé (1836–1911) confronted Jameson, en route for Johannesburg, and forced him to surrender himself and his 500 followers after pathetic resistance. The anticipated rising never materialized. Jameson, his supporters and the other Uitlanders involved in the conspiracy were shown leniency by the authorities in Pretoria and handed over to Cape officials. However, the incident served to increase

Boer suspicions of British skullduggery. Nor were these suspicions entirely misplaced. Chamberlain had had knowledge of Jameson's plan for a coup, and had provided land to Jameson's company in Bechuanaland – the staging ground from which the raid began. The Colonial Secretary himself harbored a strong interest in a united South Africa under British control, a fact of which both Boer republics were aware.

Rhodes was obliged to resign as Prime Minister of the Cape Colony but retained control of his company's charter by threatening to publish telegrams implicating Chamberlain in the plot if the charter were withdrawn. Jameson, the obvious scapegoat for what amounted to a wider conspiracy stretching from London to Cape Town, was imprisoned in Britain for 15 months. Chamberlain denied any involvement in the fiasco and managed to retain his post. But the damage had been done: Kruger and his government knew very well that, had Jameson succeeded, the feat would have been hailed as a triumph in London and measures would have been taken to annex the Transvaal – a reprise of 1877. The raid led to support from the Orange Free State where hitherto there existed no defensive agreement between the Boer republics; and it strengthened ties with the Cape Boers, many of whom supported the Afrikaner Bond, an anti-British political organization.

The raid also aggravated already tense relations between Britain and Germany. Kaiser Wilhelm II (1859–1941) saw fit to congratulate the Kruger Government in a telegram, thinly disguising his joy at Britain's humiliation. The communication fueled the jingoists in Britain and bolstered the Boers' (as it turned out, mistaken) belief that in any future conflict with Britain the republics could rely on foreign assistance.

The path towards open confrontation between London and Pretoria grew clearer. As the future Prime Minister of South Africa, Jan Smuts (1870–1950), would later write:

The Jameson Raid was the real declaration of war in the Anglo-Boer conflict ... [The] aggressors consolidated their alliance ... the defenders on the other hand silently and grimly prepared for the inevitable.

Opposing forces

British and Imperial forces

The two sides were far from equally matched. In theory at least, the British Army had the advantage. At the outbreak of war, however, the advantage lay with the Boers. Their knowledge of the terrain, presence on the ground, superior mobility and familiarity with the climate were all immediate strengths which the British could not at once surpass. On the other hand, once mustered, the power of Britain and her empire was immense. First, Britain possessed complete command of the sea, enabling it to supply the Cape Colony and Natal unhindered (provided, of course, that Durban remained beyond the Boers' reach), albeit at a considerable distance from home. Moreover, her naval position enabled her to cut off the already land-locked Boer republics from access to the sea, depriving them of all seaborne supplies and foreign aid. Quite

apart from the manpower to be derived from a nation of approximately 41 million, Britain could draw on troops willingly supplied by her empire – the largest in the world – including Australians, New Zealanders, Canadians, and others, as well as volunteers from the Cape and Natal. Weapons, food, medical supplies and all the other sinews of war could be obtained in vast quantities.

At 106,000 men, the British Army was not large by the standards of other European states. It was, however, highly professional and possessed extensive combat experience after 60 years' campaigning throughout the world fighting a host of colonial adversaries

Fit to fight? In the process of examining hundreds of thousands of largely urban, working-class men as potential recruits, the army discovered such a shocking level of health and fitness that it had to reject almost one-third of the men on the basis of their poor physical condition. (Ann Ronan Picture Library)

including Afghans, Zulus, Maoris, Egyptians, Dervishes, and Sikhs. Reserves accounted for another 75,000 men, but a large proportion of the army was based overseas, scattered across the world. Indeed, in the middle of 1899, British forces in Natal and the Cape numbered only about 10,000 men. It was not until 8 September that the Cabinet decided to double that strength, drawing half the reinforcements from garrisons in India. On 22 September the War Office mobilized an army corps of 47,000 men to be dispatched to South Africa, but at the outbreak of war in October British forces still stood at only 14,000 men.

Until the arrival of reinforcements, the Boers not only outnumbered their adversaries, but consisted almost entirely of mounted troops, while the British infantry – the bulk of the army – had no idea of the sort of fighting into which they were about to be thrown. With scant knowledge of local topography and virtually no accurate maps, the British, albeit with great *potential* power, began the war under trying circumstances. Materiel, as well as manpower, was slow to reach full strength. Stringent economies in the army in recent years meant that weapons, ammunition, horse equipment, transport and other essential articles were insufficient for anything beyond small-scale operations. As soon as campaigning began, stocks of all manner of things ran short.

The British Army at least appeared appropriately dressed for this campaign. The army had only just adopted new campaign dress in 1897, exchanging its long-cherished scarlet jackets for khaki, a light-colored brown, the word derived from the Hindustani for 'dust'. That this change had been so long in coming speaks volumes about the importance of tradition and the inherent conservatism of the institution. At long last War Office officials had heeded the call of experienced field officers for proper camouflage, headgear suited to the climate, and loose, durable materials. A few concessions were made to tradition: all Scottish Highland regiments, for instance, continued to wear their traditional tartan kilts, sporrans and other attendant garments, but with khaki aprons to cover the distinctive colors. All arms – infantry, cavalry, artillery, and engineers – wore the same white cork foreign-service helmet, covered with khaki material and often bearing the distinctive band of cotton cloth around its middle, known as the 'puggree'.

Yet the simple adoption of khaki did not entirely conceal the 'Tommy' in the bleak landscape. Immediate and tragic experience – the shocking and costly losses suffered in the opening months of the war – obliged British commanders to adopt new tactics, formations and weapons, as well as to make radical alterations to uniforms, stripping them of distinguishing colors, helmet flashes, marks of rank and bright accoutrements, and prompting General Methuen to complain that he looked like a second-class bus conductor. All such changes were deemed necessary in order to fight a largely unseen enemy whom the more foolish of observers continued to regard with snobbish contempt long after the Boers' fighting prowess ought to have dispelled the myth that they were mere yokels waiting to be swept aside by British bayonets.

At the outbreak of the conflict the infantry regiments which accounted for the vast majority of British forces mostly still carried the bolt-action Lee-Metford rifle, a weapon which was undergoing replacement by the improved model, the Lee-Enfield. Its maximum range was 1,800 m (2,000 yards), though it was at its most effective at under half that distance. Each regiment of infantry and cavalry had two Maxim machine guns in support. These were impressive weapons, firing 600 rounds a minute to a maximum range of 1,800 m (2,000 yards).

Cavalry regiments carried the carbine (a shortened version of the standard infantry weapon), a bandolier containing 50 rounds of ammunition, and a more or less obsolete sword. Numerous mounted infantry regiments, who would reach the battlefield on horseback but fight on foot, were raised in large numbers after commanders began to appreciate the crucial role that mobility was

to play in this highly fluid conflict. The mounted infantry were armed and equipped like the cavalry. Lancers carried in addition their own specialized weapon, a steel-tipped 2.75 m (9 foot) bamboo shaft. Like their counterparts in the infantry, most cavalry officers carried a pistol, though as this distinguished them from the ordinary ranks, marking them out as special targets, some opted for the ordinary carbine.

The artillery was composed of batteries of six guns each, 12-pound breach-loading guns for the horse artillery, which enjoyed extra mobility from large horse-teams, and 15-pounders for the ordinary field batteries. Standard ordnance came in several forms. Shrapnel consisted of a shell containing lead balls which, when fired over its target, to a maximum range of 3,600 m (4,000 yards), exploded, sending the projectiles showering down in a cone. The artillery also fired the new high-explosive lyddite shell, which could be propelled somewhat further than its shrapnel counterpart. Siege batteries, eventually available in substantial numbers, consisted of 5-inch howitzers.

British forces crossing the Tugela River with a 4.7 inch naval gun. The shortage of field batteries was partly alleviated by the employment of naval artillery which was landed from ships offshore, fitted with carriages and dispatched to the front. Without these guns Ladysmith probably would have fallen. (Ann Ronan Picture Library)

The British Army was supported by a number of volunteer, mounted colonial units, largely raised in the Cape Colony from among the loyal inhabitants, as well as from Uitlander refugees from the Free State and Transvaal. Uniforms and equipment sometimes followed the British standard, but the distinctive slouch hat was particularly favored. There were also a number of volunteer units raised in Britain, some of which attracted thousands of recruits. The Imperial Yeomanry, for instance, was formed at this time, and was made up of volunteers from existing yeomanry regiments – home-defense units which themselves could not be sent abroad – to increase the forces available to be deployed in South Africa. Beginning in 1900, British forces were also bolstered by large volunteer, usually mounted, contingents from the self-governing colonies of Australia (16,600), New Zealand (6,300), and Canada (7,300).

Lady Minto, wife of the British High Commissioner in Canada, presenting colours to Herchmer's Horse, an irregular volunteer unit, as they leave Ottawa for service in South Africa, 19 January 1900. (Ann Ronan Picture Library)

Boer forces

The stereotypical image of the Boer fighter as a hard-bitten, hard-riding, crack shot, proof against all weather conditions and capable of living off the poorest of rations drawn directly from the land, has some basis in fact, but by the turn of the 20th century many Boers no longer lived the rural or semi-nomadic existences of their forebears of two generations earlier. They were, however, generally tough, well-motivated, self-reliant, determined men, skilled with firearms and accustomed to hard lives on the veld, some with experience of fighting native Africans on the frontiers. Discipline was seldom a problem, not least under circumstances in which most Boers believed they were fighting to preserve their way of life. At least during the initial stages of the war their familiarity with the terrain and climate gave

them a natural advantage over the typical 'Khaki'. Winston Churchill (1874–1965), sent to the front as a correspondent for the *Daily Mail*, was by no means alone in his respect and admiration for the fighting ability of the Boers, as his recollection shows:

What men they were, these Boers! ... Thousands of independent riflemen, thinking for themselves, possessed of beautiful weapons, led with skill, living as they rode without commissariat or transport or ammunition column, moving like the wind ...

Boer forces possessed nothing like the formal structure of their opponents and, with the ability to mobilize in a matter of days, they were more or less permanently ready to be deployed in the field. The bulk of Boer forces were organized into 'commandos', small units whose strengths varied from a few hundred to several thousand men, generally connected with particular towns or regions. A burgher, once mobilized, was therefore said to be 'on commando'. Every man between the ages of 16 and 60, with the occasional exception, was obliged to serve without pay

Louis Botha, an ordinary burgher at the start of the war, through distinguished service he rapidly came to play a decisive part in the Boer victories at Colenso, Spion Kop, and Vaalkrans. He succeeded to senior command of Transvaal forces on the death of Joubert in March 1900, carrying on until the end of the war. (Ann Ronan Picture Library)

when called, but they were not constrained to join the local commando and could choose another.

Most men volunteered; compulsion was almost unheard of. These were genuinely citizen soldiers, who were expected to furnish – at their own expense – the first 10 days' rations, their own horse, a rifle and 30 rounds of ammunition. In keeping with the extremely informal nature of their defense forces, the Boers did not wear uniforms, just their ordinary clothes. In the course of the war, as their own clothes wore out, many availed themselves of captured uniforms, an offense for which the British regularly meted out the death sentence.

In striking contrast to European armies, commandos elected their own officers, including the senior officer – the commandant – and some junior ranks, all in keeping with the democratic, individualistic nature of a frontier society. Decisions were made democratically by *krygsraads*, or war councils, a process which enabled the men to choose a course of action by vote. Even more extraordinary, men could not be compelled to remain in the field, and could elect to go on leave (officially, only after three months' service) when they chose – with or without permission – a system which made it virtually impossible for senior commanders to estimate the strength of their forces. Their reasons for taking leave were sundry, but were generally confined to managing their farms or obtaining rest. Nevertheless, individual burghers seldom rode off prior to imminent action, though many might do so after an engagement.

The Boer forces were well armed. When the commandos left for the front, they did so for the most part in possession of the German 7 mm Mauser rifle, which used smokeless powder, rendering the marksman in the distance almost undetectable. The Mauser contained a clip holding five rounds, all of which could be loaded at one time, giving it an advantage over the standard British weapon, the Lee-Metford. Its magazine held ten rounds, but these had to be loaded manually one round at a time. The Mauser had a maximum range of 1,800 m (2,000 yards). Ammunition was carried in bandoliers, usually containing 60 rounds. Most Boers, having been raised on the veld, were experienced hunters and therefore competent in handling firearms under local conditions.

What rendered the Boers particularly formidable fighters was their horsemanship. Every man supplied his own horse, an animal of exceptional toughness that completely outmatched its British counterpart in its capacity to endure scorching heat by day and bitter cold by night, to carry its rider over immense distances, and to subsist on grass poor in nutrients and moisture. With every rifleman mounted, the Boers possessed a degree of mobility that the British could not hope to match, a considerable advantage in a theater of operations approximately the size of France, and with Boer forces never exceeding 60,000 at any one time.

Boer officers. Although they lacked a military air and appearance, ragged, undisciplined civilians such as these nevertheless proved formidable opponents and kept a professional army at bay for nearly three years. While only lightly armed with rifles and bandoliers, the Boers were well-mounted, toughened to the climate and fighting on familiar ground. (Ann Ronan Picture Library)

Both republics possessed a professional artillery arm, well equipped with recently acquired modern field pieces from the Krupp factories in Germany and from Creusot in France. The Transvaal artillery, including reservists, numbered about 650 men, while the Free State had about 400. Between the two republics they could muster about 100 guns crewed by well-trained men who were often commanded by experienced foreign officers. Although the Boers had fewer guns than their adversaries, their weapons enjoyed greater range than their counterparts in the Royal Artillery and, to compensate, the British were obliged to employ naval guns. The Boers had four 150 mm Creusot siege guns, later known as 'Long Toms' and four 120 mm Krupp howitzers. The bulk of their pieces were 75 mm field guns, 65 mm mountain guns, light but quick-firing 'pom poms' and about 30 Maxim machine guns.

An often forgotten contribution to the Boer military effort was made by the black African servants who served in the field as *agterryers* ('after-riders'). They performed a number of functions, including cooking, digging entrenchments, hunting, driving wagons, and the holding of spare horses. There were also many soldiers of foreign descent fighting on the Boer side. These formed themselves into volunteer bodies sometimes designated 'corps' or 'brigades', consisting of French, Italians, Dutch, Germans, Americans, Irish and other nationalities, unpaid though supplied with weapons and equipment by the republics.

Various estimates exist for the size of the Boer forces at the start of the war, but they appeared to number no more than 85,000, of which approximately 41,000 Transvaalers and about 27,000 Free Staters were immediately available for the field. The two republics had eventually between them about 2,600 men in the regular artillery and the paramilitary mounted police, with approximately another 2,000 in foreign corps. In the Cape there were about 40,000 Afrikaner men of fighting age, approximately 13,000 of whom are thought to have borne arms for the republican cause.

Spoiling for a fight

Rhodes's resignation as Prime Minister of the Cape Colony in the wake of the Jameson Raid did not allay Boer concerns. Indeed, in the Cape itself the substantial Boer population felt a deeper connection than ever to their brethren to the north, while the Orange Free State, seeing the Jameson Raid as a threat to its security, renewed its 1887 alliance with the Transvaal in March 1897, by which the two countries pledged to assist one another against any external threat. Both republics now began to make large purchases of arms and ammunition from Germany and France in preparation for possible confrontation with Britain.

Although the law required every Transvaaler to own a rifle, it was soon discovered that only half of the burghers actually had firearms, and that they were so short of ammunition that, in the event of war, stocks would be expended within a fortnight. Kruger immediately placed orders for 37,000 Mauser rifles from Germany and large quantities of heavy artillery. By the time the war broke out the Transvaal had imported 80,000 of the latest rifles and 80 million rounds of ammunition, and had re-equipped its army with the best French and German artillery available.

The Boer republics had good reason to suspect British motives, as British interests in the Transvaal rested not only on the economic grounds discussed earlier, but on important strategic grounds, as well. Since the 1870s Europe had been gripped by a new wave of colonial enthusiasm. Britain had emerged as the dominant power, particularly in South Africa, where the Cape Colony served a key function in protecting the trade route to India, Singapore, Burma, and Hong Kong.

Quite apart from national and geo-strategic concerns, there were also individual interests at stake. Rhodes, at least temporarily marginalized from the political scene, was not alone in his desire to see the British flag fly over the Boer republics. Chamberlain, a staunch imperialist convinced of British cultural superiority, strongly supported Uitlander claims for a political voice. Their grievances appeared to justify British interference in the internal affairs of the Transvaal.

Chamberlain employed two methods to achieve his aims: he planned first to make demands on Pretoria that would oblige the Kruger Government to concur and so humiliate it, and second, to claim that the Transvaal did not enjoy complete independence, but must defer to Britain on at least one crucial point: foreign affairs. In this respect the Colonial Secretary could refer to the London Convention, specifically Article IV, which prevented the conclusion of treaties with foreign powers, apart from the Orange Free State, without prior approval from Britain. This, in Chamberlain's view, placed the Transvaal in a subordinate position, and he extended his interpretation of what constituted foreign affairs to include three laws of which he disapproved: the Aliens Expulsion Law, the Immigration Law and the Press Law, all of which were designed to keep the influence of Uitlanders in check.

In May 1897, Chamberlain appointed Sir Alfred Milner (1854–1924) as High Commissioner for South Africa. Milner came to play a crucial role in the months preceding the war. If the Jameson Raid had set Britain and the Boer republics on the road to conflict, it was Milner's arrival in South Africa that rapidly accelerated the pace, for he and Kruger would develop an intense personal dislike for one another. Oxford-educated, intelligent and

Sir Alfred Milner, Governor of the Cape Colony and British High Commissioner for South Africa. As the Crown's key representative on the ground, Milner bears much of the responsibility for precipitating the crisis which rapidly degenerated into war. (Ann Ronan Picture Library)

conspiratorial, Milner had served in an administrative capacity in Egypt and was as committed an imperialist as Chamberlain himself. He shared the Colonial Secretary's desire for a united, British, South Africa. Although the Orange Free State and the Transvaal had no plans for unification, Afrikaner nationalism had been aroused by the Jameson Raid, and Milner feared that, in the event of war, the Boer population in the Cape might rise in support of their brethren.

Evidence of Boer solidarity and confirmation of these fears emerged when Kruger was re-elected President of the Transvaal by an overwhelming majority in February 1898. Thereafter Milner was bent on

provoking the Transvaal into a crisis with Britain over the question of Uitlander's rights, in order to justify armed intervention. In fact he adopted a tough line in all matters concerning the Transvaal, convinced that Kruger stood in the way of progressive reform, of capitalism, and of the growth of the empire. Writing to Chamberlain a few days after the election, Milner stated ominously:

There is no way out of the political troubles except reform in the Transvaal or war ... I should be inclined to work up to a crisis ... by steadily and inflexibly pressing for the redress of substantial wrongs ... It means we shall have to fight.

But, at least for the moment, the Government in London did not wish to adopt a belligerent policy; Chamberlain therefore urged further negotiation.

It will be recalled that Kruger had extended the period of residence for enfranchisement from five to 14 years. This was probably an unnecessary step, however, as Uitlanders were, for the most part, not interested in citizenship or the right to vote. They were largely concerned about continued residence and low taxes. The real threat and the source of most of the grievances over political rights came from the wealthier members of the Uitlander community, in particular the mining magnates and their companies. They possessed justifiable grounds for claiming that the Transvaal Government had substantially raised the cost of mining operations, and that various concessions and monopolies had been offered to particular companies, thereby preventing free enterprise and open competition.

Tension rose in December 1898 when a British national, Tom Edgar, was shot by a Transvaal constable. The pro-Uitlander South African League protested vigorously, while Milner, in London at the time, was discussing the action to be taken against the Transvaal. On his return in early 1899 he sent back reports exaggerating problems between the Pretoria Government and the Uitlanders, carefully preparing the ground for both the Cabinet and the British public at large to confront the Boers on behalf of their apparently oppressed compatriots.

Milner went so far as to forward a petition to Queen Victoria herself in March 1899, containing the signatures of 22,000 Uitlanders demanding assistance in securing the franchise. To Milner, such an appeal justified intervention on behalf of subjects who, though accounting for perhaps half the population of the Transvaal, were subject to an onerous level of taxation particular to foreign residents, while simultaneously denied a political voice. He was not loath to make his thoughts known officially; on 4 May he telegraphed to Chamberlain what became known as the 'Helot's Despatch', containing an exaggerated account of the plight of the Uitlanders, and appealing for direct British intervention in the Transvaal. Thousands of British subjects lived under conditions which rendered them little more than slaves, Milner argued. For their sakes, and for the sake of British prestige and dignity, London must act. His message ran,

It is idle talk to talk of peace and unity in such a state of affairs ... The case for intervention is overwhelming ... The spectacle of thousands of British subjects kept permanently in the position of helots ... does steadily undermine the influence and reputation of Great Britain.

Milner's efforts began to pay off. Chamberlain informed Kruger by dispatch that the Queen looked with concern on the grievances of her subjects in the Transvaal. In effect, Pretoria was being put on notice: either fundamental political reform was to be undertaken, or war would ensue.

Efforts now began to stave off conflict through the offices of two moderate leaders in the region: President Marthinus Steyn (1857–1916) of the Orange Free State and W. P. Schreiner, Rhodes's successor as Prime Minister of the Cape Colony. Steyn hosted a conference in Bloemfontein to which he invited Milner and Kruger. During the course of the discussions, which lasted from 31 May to 5 June, Kruger offered to grant the Uitlanders the vote after seven years' residence instead of 14, but in return he expected substantial concessions: the annexation of Swaziland by the Orange Free State, compensation for the costs connected with the Jameson Raid and new talks to clarify the points contained in the London Convention. Milner, who had every intention of seeing the conference fail, rejected these concessions, proposing five years' residency as the qualification for suffrage. Kruger indignantly refused. As Milner withdrew from the conference on 5 June, without authorization from London, Kruger accurately and bitterly asserted: 'It is our country you want.'

With the failure of the Bloemfontein Conference, events rapidly accelerated towards war. Milner believed that nothing short of conflict would enable Britain to remain the dominant power in South Africa. Further talks on the Uitlander question repeatedly failed, and with confrontation

Marthinus Steyn, President of the Orange Free State. Steyn opposed the war in 1899 and mediated between Kruger and Milner to try to avert it. Once hostilities began, however, he was fully committed to the struggle and became a staunch 'bitter-ender'. (Ann Ronan Picture Library)

apparently inevitable, Milner requested the immediate dispatch of 10,000 troops to South Africa. Boer leaders, who distrusted Chamberlain as much as they did Milner, began to see war as inevitable. Nevertheless, for a short time a breakthrough seemed possible. In mid-July the Volksraad, the Parliament of the Transvaal, passed legislation lowering to seven years the residency requirement for the enfranchisement of Uitlanders. In London, the House of Commons proposed to study the altered situation, but on 28 July Chamberlain went further in securing Parliament's support for war in the event that it deemed such reforms unacceptable.

Bowing to pressure, in August and September Kruger offered various new concessions, including reducing residency to five years provided that Britain withdrew its claim to suzerainty. Milner condemned Kruger's conditions in his dispatches to Chamberlain, and partly as a result of Milner's stance, London rejected the compromise. Various jingoistic newspapers in London were beginning to sound the trumpets for war. Both sides made increasingly belligerent and provocative speeches, and with weapons now arriving in the Boer republics from abroad, Chamberlain decided to take a hard line. On 8 September the War Office dispatched the 10,000 troops Milner had requested, drawn from the British garrisons in India, Egypt, Cyprus and Malta.

On 22 September, the decision for war having been made, the British Government

Commandant-General Piet Joubert, the senior Transvaal commander in the early months of the war. His cardinal error was his refusal, despite the repeated pleas of his subordinates, to follow up his victory at Modderspruit on 30 October 1899 by pursuing the British before they took refuge in Ladysmith. (Ann Ronan Picture Library)

drew up an ultimatum for Kruger, to be presented once all troop dispositions were complete. The Transvaal and her ally, the Orange Free State, did not remain inactive during this build-up. On 27 September Commandant-General Piet Joubert (1831–1900) mobilized just over half the Transvaal commandos and deployed them on the borders. On 2 October, President Steyn, who had sought to maintain peace, followed suit, faithful to his agreement of March 1897.

October is early spring in South Africa. The veld grass had grown sufficiently to support the animals on which the Boer forces absolutely depended: the horses on which every rifleman rode, the oxen that hauled the wagon trains, and the cattle on which the burghers fed. Kruger was thus able to take the fateful step of issuing an ultimatum on 9 October demanding a settlement by arbitration of all points in dispute between Britain and the Transvaal. Several unacceptable clauses were deliberately included, these among others:

That the troops on the borders of the Republic shall be instantly withdrawn. That all reinforcements of troops which have arrived in South Africa since 1 July, 1899, shall be removed. That Her Majesty's troops which are now on the high seas shall not be landed in any part of South Africa.

Finally, if Britain refused to comply within 48 hours, the Transvaal would consider itself formally at war.

Before dawn on 10 October Chamberlain received news of the ultimatum with joy. 'They have done it!' he exclaimed, relieved that by his action Kruger had placed the onus of war on the Transvaal, thereby freeing the British Government from having to issue an ultimatum of its own. The fact that the Transvaal and, by extension, its ally the Orange Free State, had cast itself as the aggressor was certain to galvanize widespread domestic support in Britain. There the Government rejected the ultimatum without hesitation and war with the two Boer republics began on 11 October 1899.

When, years later, Deneys Reitz, a former Boer soldier and future South African politician, reflected on the final period of crisis which led to hostilities, he offered some sound arguments in support of the widely-held view that war was inevitable:

I have no doubt that the British Government had made up its mind to force the issue, and was the chief culprit, but the Transvaalers were also spoiling for a fight, and, from what I saw in Pretoria during the few weeks that preceded the ultimatum, I feel sure that the Boers would in any case have insisted on a rupture.

Briton versus Boer

The Boer offensive

When war began Britain had only about 14,000 men in Natal, with the 1st Army Corps of 47,000 men being mobilized in Britain. Aware of their temporary advantage over an opponent with enormous potential power, the Boers sensibly assumed the offensive. The experience of the conflict of 1880–81 doubtless contributed to this decision. The Boers hoped to inflict a rapid series of victories in Natal and the Cape Colony. By employing this bold strategy they sought to force the British to negotiate a quick settlement to the war before the full resources of their empire could be brought to bear against the two republics. The main objective was to isolate or destroy British troops poised for invasion on their borders. Next, Boer forces were to proceed into Natal and the Cape in order to prevent the movement of British reinforcements from the coast.

In the west, the Boers again seized the initiative. On this front Assistant Commandant-General Piet Cronjé, with 7,000 men, concentrated on two principal objectives, the first involving a thrust against Kimberley, in Natal, near the border with the Orange Free State. By 3 November, 4,800 Free State burghers under Chief-Commandant C. J. Wessels, and 2,200 Transvaalers under Assistant Commandant-General Koos de la Rey (1847–1914), had completely encircled the town, which was being held by 2,600 men under Colonel Robert Kekewich (1854–1914). It happened that the arch-rival of the Boers, Cecil Rhodes, was trapped in the town. On the same front but further to the north, De la Rey's men captured an armored train at Kraaipan – the first action of the war – on the evening of 12 October, and the following day completely surrounded Mafeking, with Colonel Robert Baden-Powell (1857–1941) in command of a mere 1,000 whites and 300 armed blacks. In the south another arm of the offensive extended into the Cape Colony, where the Boers hoped to encourage Cape Afrikaners to flock to the republics' aid, either to join the Boer ranks, or to foment revolt against Crown authority.

The main Boer thrust, however, was made into Natal, where the principal forces of the Transvaal, together with contingents from the Orange Free State, rode through Laing's Nek, a pass in the Drakensberg range connecting the Transvaal and Natal and leading towards Durban, the vital port at which the first British reinforcements were expected to land. The largest concentration of British troops in South Africa was, in fact, in Natal: 9,600 under Lieutenant-General Sir George White (1835–1912), Commander-in-Chief of the forces in that colony and based at Ladysmith, the second largest town in the colony, and 4,500 under General Sir William Penn Symons (1843–99) at Dundee, in northern Natal. The Boers, meanwhile, under Commandant-General Piet Joubert, had 11,400 Transvaalers and 6,000 men from the Free State deployed on the Natal front. Joubert had as his prime objective the defeat of Penn Symons's troops at Dundee opening the way to Ladysmith, which stood at the railway junction between the Orange Free State, the Transvaal and Natal.

The first battle of the war took place at Talana Hill, outside Dundee, on 20 October. Seeking to block the Boers' progress, Penn Symons launched his men up the rocky slopes of the hill. Captain Nugent of the 60th, who was hit three times in this action, described the ground as 'strewn with bodies'. Despite heavy losses, the attack succeeded, driving off the Boers under

General Lucas Meyer (1846–1902). Though technically a defeat for the Boers, the fact that Penn Symons was mortally wounded, with the loss of 447 British soldiers killed to the Boers' paltry 150, immediately demonstrated that the Boers were not only well armed but also skilled marksmen. Penn Symons had employed traditional tactics – preparatory artillery bombardment, followed by a frontal infantry assault, and finally a cavalry charge – tactics that were to prove outmoded in nearly all subsequent actions. As the Boers did not retire far, Penn Symons's successor, Major-General James Yule (1847–1920), decided that Dundee was not worth defending, and prepared to abandon it in favor of Ladysmith, in central Natal.

As the troops evacuated Dundee and proceeded south amidst a ferocious thunderstorm, White engaged the pursuing Free State commandos at Elandslaagte, near Ladysmith, on 21 October, clearing them

from a series of kopjes before unleashing his lancers on them as they fled. Boer losses were more serious than at Talana, with 336 casualties, of which 46, including their mortally wounded commander, Assistant Commandant-General J. H. Kock (1835–99), were killed, but British losses were heavy yet again: 213 wounded and 50 killed. The battle is noteworthy for the involvement that day of three British officers who were later to take leading parts in the First World War: Major-General John French (1852–1925), who commanded the cavalry; Major Douglas Haig (1861–1928), French's Chief of Staff; and Colonel Ian Hamilton (1853–1947), who commanded the infantry. The fact that traditional tactics involving the bayonet and cavalry charges were largely responsible for the Boer rout may well have lulled the British into the deeply mistaken impression that conventional methods would thereafter inevitably sweep the Boers from the field.

White now made the cardinal mistake of failing to pursue the defeated Boers. Instead he chose to concentrate his troops, thus allowing the Transvaalers under Joubert the opportunity to occupy a series of hills ringing Ladysmith. Seeking to prevent the encirclement, White

Charge of the 5th Lancers at the Battle of Elandslaagte, 21 October 1899. No quarter was offered. One British officer described the scene thus: 'We went along sticking our lances through them – it was a terrible thing, but you have to do it…'. (Ann Ronan Picture Library)

planned a night attack against Pepworth Hill and Nicholson's Nek on 29–30 October. Misunderstandings, compounded by darkness, prevented White from dislodging the Boers from their concealed positions on the hills. When dawn arrived his men were left exposed to heavy fire, bringing a swift end to the attack. Losses totaled 1,764 killed and wounded, and White was forced to retreat into Ladysmith. The town was hardly equipped to accommodate such large numbers: 13,000 troops, together with their 2,500 servants, joined the 5,400 residents, all packed into a small area surrounded by hills on which Boer artillery stood secure from attack. With hindsight, White was heavily criticized for failing to establish a defensive position along the Tugela River.

On the southern and south-western fronts, again the Boers assumed the offensive, but they deployed only about 3,000 men and took just one of the three strategically important railway junctions. It was not until the middle of November that Chief-Commandant J. H.

Olivier forced the British back to Queenstown, while General Schoeman reached only as far as Colesberg and neglected to leave troops at the railway junctions at Naauwpoort and De Aar, thereby leaving much of the railway system in British hands.

During November the Boer offensive gradually lost its momentum and a substantial proportion of the troops were occupied in long and ineffective sieges. By splitting their forces and tying troops down at Kimberley, Ladysmith and Mafeking, Joubert and Cronjé lost the opportunity to strike deep into Natal and the Cape Colony while British forces were numerically inferior and scattered. A fine opportunity offered itself, however, for with White trapped in

Assistant Commandant-General Piet Cronjé, who commanded Boer forces in the western Transvaal at the outbreak of war. He initiated the siege of Mafeking, and opposed Lord Methuen's attempts to relieve Kimberley at the Modder River and Magersfontein. Disaster ultimately befell Cronjé in February 1900, when he was forced to surrender a large force. (Ann Ronan Picture Library)

Principal theaters of operations, battles and sieges

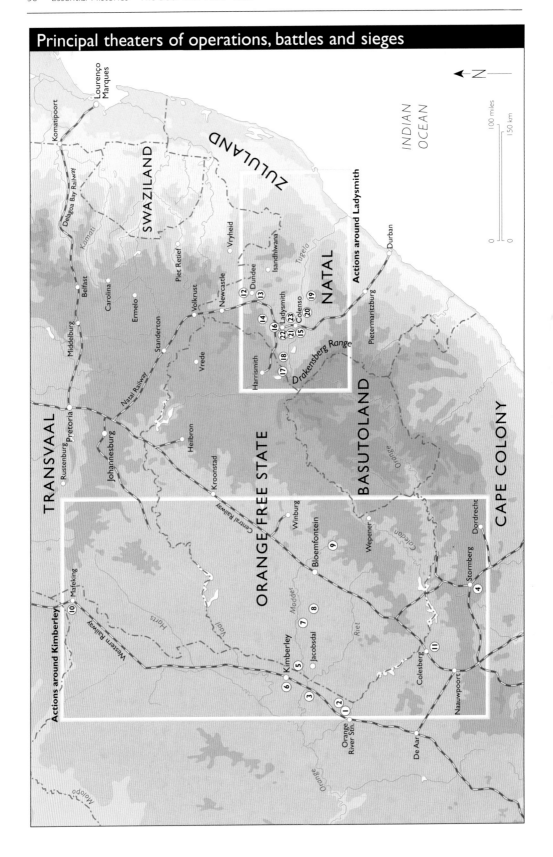

Ladysmith, Natal lay open to further incursions, and any thrust against Durban might have denied the British the vital base through which their troops and supplies from around the world passed. In the south, the Boers had failed to seize all the vital railway junctions, thus enabling the British, once in a position to launch an offensive of their own, to advance north through the Cape.

Despite the British success at Elandslaagte, the Boers managed to surround Ladysmith, the second largest town in Natal, trapping White and approximately 10,000 men. The Boers, under Joubert and Botha, made one major attempt to break into the town's defenses when, on 6 January 1900, they gathered 5,000 men for an assault against the southern sector, held by Ian Hamilton. Hamilton himself launched several sorties, losing heavily to a storm of Boer rifle fire. Yet the Boer assault also failed, leaving a stalemate. During January and February morale declined, typhoid fever killed nearly 400 people and food began to run short. A relief column under Buller finally reached the town after scoring a victory at Pieter's Hill on 27 February.

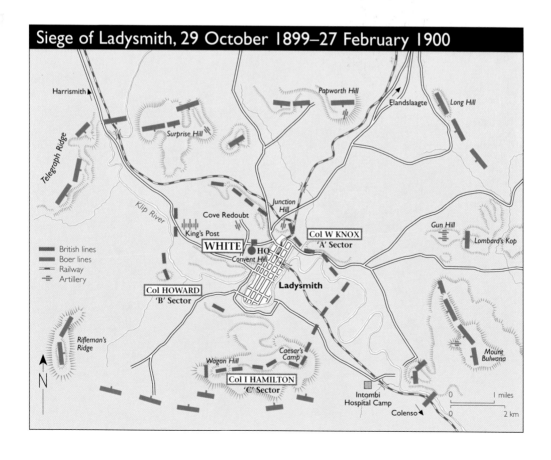

Siege of Ladysmith, 29 October 1899–27 February 1900

Lieutenant-General Sir George White. A veteran of the Indian Mutiny, Second Afghan War, and the campaign in the Sudan, White led the Natal Field Force, which became bottled up in Ladysmith. His successful defense went largely unrewarded. (Ann Ronan Picture Library)

Buller's offensive

The Boers' failure to inflict an early knock-out blow, and in particular to gain mastery over important ports such as Durban, arguably cost them the war. The 47,000 men of the British 1st Corps continued their journey to South Africa, where safe points of disembarkation awaited them.

Accompanying this formidable contingent was the new Commander-in-Chief of British forces in South Africa, General Sir Redvers Buller (1839–1908), a large, stocky, gruff hero of the Zulu War in whom both the British

Government and public placed a great deal of confidence. On his arrival at Cape Town on 31 October, Buller received news of White's loss of most of northern Natal and of the investments of Ladysmith, Kimberley and Mafeking. This unforeseen situation frustrated his original plan: his troops having landed at Cape Town, Port Elizabeth and East London, they were originally supposed to converge on the Orange River, from which Buller planned to launch an offensive up the railway line through the Orange Free State, take the capital, Bloemfontein, and then invade the Transvaal to capture Pretoria. Instead, concerned that the loss of the besieged towns would badly damage British prestige, he sought to relieve Ladysmith and Kimberley as quickly as possible, and to put a halt to the Boer offensive in Natal and the northern Cape.

General Sir Redvers Buller. Commander-in-Chief of British forces in South Africa during the first months of the war, he rapidly fell out of favor as a result of his costly, though ultimately successful, attempts to relieve Ladysmith at Colenso, Spion Kop, Vaalkrans and Tugela Heights. (Ann Ronan Picture Library)

To do so Buller chose to divide his force – as the Boers had done for their own offensive – though in this case into three parts. Lieutenant-General Lord Methuen (1845–1932), in command of a small field force, was to march beside the western railway line to try to relieve Kimberley, while the second element, under General Francis Clery (1838–1926), then at Colesberg, and Lieutenant-General Sir William Gatacre (1843–1906), near Stormberg, was to drive the Boer forces which had penetrated into the Cape Colony back across the Orange River. Buller himself planned to retake northern Natal and relieve Ladysmith using half the total troops at his disposal.

In the meantime, following the sieges of Kimberley, Mafeking and Ladysmith, the Boer offensive rapidly fizzled out. Overruling the objections of the younger, bolder leaders, Joubert refused to take any risks, authorizing instead only a minor raid into Natal. With 2,000 burghers, he carried out reconnaissance as far as Estcourt, in order to discover points at which to establish the strong defense necessary to block the advance of British reinforcements from the coast. The only other action of note occurred on 15 November, when a commando under Assistant Commandant-General Louis Botha (1862–1919) captured an armored train near Chieveley by blocking the line with boulders. The British lost two men and 20 were badly injured. The young war correspondent, Winston Churchill, was among the 50 prisoners taken to Pretoria, whence he made a daring escape a few weeks later, reaching friendly lines on foot and on a coal truck.

During this period of relative inaction the British reorganized and by the end of November, just as Buller was arriving at Durban, Methuen, with 10,000 men, was poised for an offensive in the west. He intended to relieve Kimberley as quickly as possible. Following the railway line through the northern Cape with 10,500 men and continuous arrivals of reinforcements, he

Battle of Belmont, 23 November 1899, the first major action on the western front. Seeking to relieve Kimberley, Methuen first had to drive Free State burghers from several kopjes blocking his advance. Shown here, the 1st Guards Brigade launches a successful bayonet attack. (Ann Ronan Picture Library)

scored two minor but costly successes against De la Rey at Belmont and Graspan, on 23 and 25 November, respectively, obliging the 3,600 Boers to retire to the line of the Modder River. At its confluence with the Reit – a position obstructing the route to Kimberley – Cronjé's men dug in, constructing slit trenches along the riverbank, with clear, open country to their front that offered an ideal, unobstructed view. Methuen, ignoring reports of a strong Boer presence and lacking accurate maps, decided on a frontal attack, set for 28 November.

So intense was the hail of Boer rifle fire that the advancing British infantry, lacking any form of cover, were forced to hug the ground, unable either to go forward or back. They remained prone for 10 hours under a blazing sun with temperatures reaching 45°C (108°F). The Scots Guards suffered particularly badly for, clad in their traditional kilts, the backs of their legs became severely burned. Lacking food and water, some tried to crawl to the supply wagons, only to be killed in the attempt. By sundown the fighting at the Modder River subsided in stalemate, with severe losses to Methuen's force – approximately 500 casualties. Nevertheless, the Boers were again

Highlanders crossing the unexpectedly swollen Modder River under fire, 28 November 1899. Methuen, ignoring reports of a strong Boer presence, foolishly remarked, 'They are not here.' Concealed riflemen soon demonstrated otherwise. (Ann Ronan Picture Library)

obliged to fall back overnight when Free Staters on the western flank under Commandant Marthinus Prinsloo (1838–1903) withdrew from their important positions, thus jeopardizing the safety of the remaining men. Taking advantage of the darkness, they rode off a few miles and occupied a new position, along a low ridge that cut across the railway line, as before, blocking the British advance to Kimberley. This was Magersfontein.

At Magersfontein, Koos de la Rey made masterful use of trenches, excavating not on the kopjes themselves, but on the plains to their front. These trenches, dug with straight sides about 1 m (1 yard) in width and the same in depth – much narrower and deeper than their British counterparts – enabled the defenders to stand upright and fire over the breastworks while concealed by camouflage fashioned from branches and grass. The Boers partially covered some trenches, providing themselves with a degree of protection against shells. While the trench had featured in both the Crimean War and the American Civil War (1861–65), it had been relegated almost exclusively to siege operations. In recognition

of the increasingly lethal nature of small arms and artillery fire, trenches were now to be employed on an ordinary battlefield – presaging the new style of warfare which was to become so familiar during the First World War only 15 years later.

After a period of regrouping and refreshing his troops, which numbered 15,000 and 33 guns, Methuen planned a second attack in his efforts to break through. He possessed no solid information on the actual position of the Boer trenches, which he erroneously believed had been dug on the hill itself rather than in front of it. Wherever they might be, and unbeknownst to Methuen, the trenches were fully occupied, for the long preparatory bombardment could not but alert the Boers to impending attack. These numbered 8,000 burghers and 10 guns under Cronjé, De la Rey having left a few days earlier to recover from a shoulder wound.

Sectional view of a typical Boer entrenchment. Although the Boers used trenches to excellent effect at the Modder River and at Magersfontein, it was only possible to construct these with sufficient time and hard work: the dry, rocky soil of South Africa contrasted sharply with the soft earth on the Western Front during the First World War. (Ann Ronan Picture Library)

Methuen opened a futile artillery bombardment of the (unoccupied) ridges on the afternoon of 10 December. Unwilling to repeat the mistake he had made at the Modder River by sending his men directly against a strong position in the cold light of day, he ordered his men forward that night under the cover of darkness. The plan went awry, however. At sunrise on 11 December his troops could be seen advancing, led by the Highland Brigade, in close formation, completely vulnerable to the repeating rifle fire of the Boers, fire which led Captain L. March Phillipps, serving in a colonial volunteer unit known as Rimington's Guides, to comment:

To advance under fire of this sort is altogether impossible. It is not a question of courage, but of the impossibility of a single man surviving ... What the devil's the use of the bravest man with half-a-dozen bullets through him?

Losses mounted at an horrendous rate. Not only was the Highland Brigade halted in its tracks in front of Magersfontein Kop, but the cavalry could make no headway to the south-east. The result was disaster: almost 950 British killed and wounded as opposed to fewer than 300 Boers. The Guards Brigade suffered particularly badly, as did the Highlanders, who lost their commanding officer, Major-General Andrew Wauchope (1846–99), a further 173 killed, and 559 wounded or missing. As at the Modder River a fortnight earlier, the British were taken by surprise, and again Kimberley would have to endure its siege that much longer. Yet unlike the previous action, the Boers remained fixed in their trenches, seemingly impossible to dislodge. Although Cronjé neglected to follow up his victory by pursuing Methuen's shattered troops, the British offensive in the west had ended in utter humiliation.

Meanwhile, near the Stormberg Junction, a railway connection of particular strategic significance on the southern front, Gatacre, with 3,000 troops, confronted 1,000 Free State forces which were attracting Cape rebels to their cause. On the night of 9–10 December, Gatacre's force set out, only to become hopelessly lost and exhausted as a

'All that was left of them': the Black Watch after the Battle of Magersfontein, by Richard Caton Woodville. Two hundred and two of 239 British killed, and 496 of 663 wounded, were Highlanders. (Ann Ronan Picture Library)

result of poor maps, darkness and unclear orders. When the sun rose on the morning of 10 December Gatacre's men were completely disorganized, and totally unprepared to defend themselves. The Boers under Chief-Commandant J. H. Olivier killed 28, wounded 51 and took 634 prisoners, at a cost of a mere 21 men to themselves.

A third reverse awaited the British. With White bottled up in Ladysmith, Joubert had undertaken reconnaissance and sought some defensible positions from which to impede the advance of British reinforcements. In late November Joubert entrenched himself in a strong position along a line of hills running behind the north bank of the Tugela near Colenso. A riding accident then left him seriously injured, and from 30 November command devolved upon Louis Botha, a leader who was to prove of exceptional energy and ability.

Buller, meanwhile, with 21,000 men, received news of Stormberg and Magersfontein just as he was approaching Botha's force of about 6,500 burghers. In the light of the other two defeats, Buller knew that he must reclaim the reputation of the army by dislodging this force, opening the road through Colenso to Ladysmith.

The attack was set for the morning of 15 December. Botha's men were well ensconced in trenches and outworks made from rock and sandbags. Buller carried out inadequate reconnaissance of these positions, made no corrections to faulty maps, and preceded the assault with two days of heavy artillery bombardment, thereby alerting the Boers to the point of attack. He had also failed to order White in Ladysmith to create a diversion in Botha's rear. Worst of all, he dismissed the recent lessons learnt and opted for the least imaginative approach: a frontal attack.

Things went badly wrong from the very start. When the action began, the artillery advanced too far ahead of the infantry and established itself too close to the Boers, attracting immediate and deadly fire. Then, Major-General Arthur Hart led the Irish Brigade in close order into a loop in the river, in search of a drift by which to effect a crossing. Disaster ensued. The brigade found itself stopped in its tracks by a storm of fire

Battle of Colenso, 15 December 1899

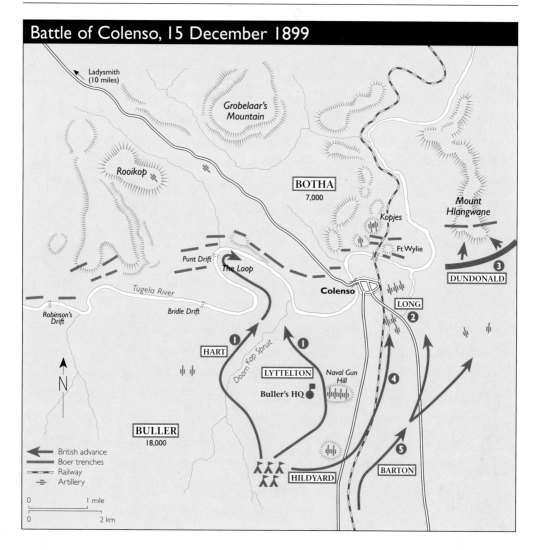

1. 6.00 am. Hart's brigade advances into the Loop to locate a known drift, exposing itself to heavy rifle fire from the front and both flanks, and from artillery. Lyttleton is sent in support, but to no avail. Unable to locate the drift, the brigades withdraw in some confusion around 7.00 am, but are not fully disengaged until 10.00 am.

2. 6.00 am. Long establishes two batteries within 1,000 yards of the river, but after suffering severe losses from rifle and shell fire, withdraws around 7.00 am, abandoning two guns to the Boers.

3. 6.00 am. Dundonald attacks Hlangwane, making early gains before being halted by heavy fire. Appeals to Barton for support go unheeded.

4. 6.30 am. Hilyard's brigade, advancing in open order and using cover, approaches Colenso. Vigorous exchange of fire with the Boers in front of Fort Wylie temporarily forces the defenders back, but lack of support obliges Hilyard to withdraw around 7.00 am.

5. Barton's brigade moves forward but remains unengaged.

against its front and both flanks by Boer riflemen concealed on the hills on the other side of the river. Private Fred Tucker of the Rifle Brigade described how 'the air seemed alive with iron and lead' and the shells 'fell within a few feet, showering us with clouds of dirt and a shrapnel [shell] burst just over our heads, the pieces falling over our bodies like acorns from a tree.'

Meanwhile, in the center, the artillery crews found themselves exposed to dreadful fire. Buller attempted to withdraw them, but it was too late. He failed to commit his reserves and, sensing an urgent need to break off the attack, limbered up his artillery and withdrew. He personally rode to the scene, calling for volunteers to rescue the guns.

Under heavy fire 10 of the 12 pieces were eventually dragged away, but at a loss of seven men and 13 horses. Among those killed was Lieutenant Freddy Roberts, son of the Field Marshal, and one of five men to be posthumously awarded the Victoria Cross for their bravery that day. Apparently losing his head, Buller ordered the troops to pull back. Sir Redvers thus earned for himself the nickname 'Sir *Reverse* Buller'. Colenso proved extremely costly: 138 British killed, 762 wounded and 220 missing or taken prisoner (about 1,100 all told) to the Boers' trifling 38.

Humiliating though Colenso was, the strategic situation in Natal remained largely unchanged, but the psychological effect, particularly at home in Britain, was tremendous. His first attempt to relieve Ladysmith having failed miserably, Buller sent a message to the War Office in London: 'My view is that I ought to let Ladysmith go, and occupy good positions for the defence of south Natal, and let time help us ... I now feel that I cannot say I can relieve Ladysmith with my available force.' He advised White by heliograph to capitulate on the best terms he could secure if he found that another month's resistance proved impossible:

Can you last long? If not, how many days can you give me in which to take up a defensive position? After which I suggest your firing away as much ammunition as you can, and making the best terms you can.

White declined the suggestion as unthinkable.

The triple disasters at Stormberg, Magersfontein, and Colenso on 10, 11 and 15 December, respectively, were of such magnitude that they came to be known collectively as 'Black Week', a source of immense consternation in Britain. Incredulity gave way to the realization that a small number of farmers could inflict telling blows against the disciplined forces of the world's greatest empire. Queen Victoria, ever a keen observer of the army's exploits, made her feelings abundantly clear: 'We are not interested in the possibilities of defeat. They do not exist.'

Saving the guns at Colenso. One of the most famous incidents of the war, in which Colonel Long's artillery advanced well ahead of supporting infantry and unlimbered in an exposed position 900 m (1,000 yards) from the Tugela. Heavy fire forced their withdrawal, though two guns had to be abandoned. (Ann Ronan Picture Library)

For military authorities in London, faulty leadership in the field stood out as the major obstacle to success. On a tactical level, Buller, Methuen and Gatacre misunderstood the realities of the new form of fighting, which consistently spelled disaster to any commander who failed to gather adequate intelligence of troop dispositions, and who recklessly sent his men forward straight into the teeth of camouflaged and entrenched positions. On the broader, strategic level, Buller's plan was fundamentally flawed. He had divided his forces, dissipating his strength and forfeiting the chance to deliver a hammer blow against a numerically inferior opponent. Finally, Buller's orders to White at Ladysmith horrified the authorities in London. All these factors prompted the War Office to dispatch a new division to South Africa immediately to reinforce the demoralized troops. As for the chastened Buller, he would remain in the field, but was to be replaced by Sir Frederick Sleigh, Lord Roberts (1832–1914) as the new supreme commander of British forces in South Africa.

For the Boers' part, they squandered another opportunity to resume the offensive with the failure of this, the first British offensive. Cronjé balked at taking risks, despite appeals made by Kruger and Steyn, backed by Vecht-General Christiaan de Wet (1854–1922) and De la Rey, to exploit recent Boer successes. Specifically, they urged him to encircle British forces in the Cape, destroy vulnerable railway lines in the rear of Methuen and Gatacre, and to seize the important railway junctions at De Aar and possibly even Naauwpoort. By declining to do so, Cronjé missed the chance to delay, if not prevent, the advance on the Free State planned by Roberts.

A lull followed Colenso, except around Ladysmith, where the Boers under General Schalk Burger (1852–1918) and Marthinus Prinsloo assembled 5,000 men and made a spirited attack against Platrand, south of the town, on 6 January 1900. The 2,000 defenders, under Ian Hamilton, launched a series of counterattacks against riflemen concealed behind rocks on a hillside, with the usual disastrous results. Seeing his men laid low under a broiling sun for no return, Hamilton eventually called a halt. The Boers, for their part, carried on the bitter struggle for the remainder of the day. The garrison courageously held off their Boer attackers, who persisted until the clouds opened and a raging thunderstorm forced them to abandon their attempts. The Boers lost approximately 250 killed and wounded.

Buller, meanwhile, still in overall command pending Roberts's arrival in South Africa, realized that he could not allow the Boers' positions on the Tugela Heights to hold up his progress. With the arrival of reinforcements which brought his forces up to 30,000 men by 23 January, he made a second attempt to force a path through and relieve Ladysmith. Determined to redeem his reputation, 'Sir Reverse' now decided to outflank a position which bitter experience had clearly shown he could not take by simple frontal assault. Upstream (west) of Colenso, about 24 km (15 miles), lay another drift, and there Buller intended to make a crossing, to be conducted by the newly arrived Lieutenant-General Sir Charles Warren (1840–1927). Granted an independent command, Warren was ordered to turn his opponents' right flank at Spion Kop ('Lookout Hill'). In the event, Warren realized that the capture of this position would render their entire line vulnerable to attack and could well open the route to Ladysmith.

Therefore, on the night of 23–24 January, just under 2,000 infantry under Major-General Edward Woodgate (1845–1900) climbed the rocky hillside and drove off the meager force defending the summit. Success, however, soon turned sour. At sunrise on the following morning the troops on the summit found themselves completely at the mercy of infantry and artillery fire directed from the other heights arrayed in a crescent looming over Spion Kop. Throughout the course of the day, confused by conflicting orders and incompetence among the senior officers, Woodgate's troops, including those seeking cover in the trenches, remained

exposed on the summit, subject to withering fire from the heights above. All the while, substantial numbers of men remained uncommitted to the fight. Casualties, including the mortally wounded Woodgate, mounted rapidly. Winston Churchill discovered evidence of the carnage as he climbed the hillside and observed the desperate need for some relief:

One thing was quite clear – unless good and efficient cover could be made during the night, and unless guns could be dragged to the summit of the hill to match the Boer artillery, the infantry could not, perhaps would not, endure another day. The human machine will not stand certain strains for long.

By dusk, his men having suffered horrific losses, Woodgate's successor, Colonel Alec Thorneycroft, ignominiously abandoned the Kop. As it happened, while the British were streaming down one side, the Boers were descending the other, only to return the following morning to

British troops manhandling artillery up Spion Kop, 24 January 1900. Thorneycroft's position on the summit became untenable when it was discovered that the Boers had deployed above them on other hills nearby. (Ann Ronan Picture Library)

reoccupy it. In the end Buller's efforts in this, the largest battle of the war, yielded nothing, and cost him another 300 killed, 1,000 wounded and 200 captured on the day of the battle alone, but about 2,000 all told since 16 January – compared to fewer than 200 Boer casualties. When the guns finally fell silent, Deneys Reitz (see 'Portrait of a soldier,' page 71), a young rifleman on commando, walked among the dead on the summit of Spion Kop:

The soldiers lay dead in swathes, and in places they were piled three deep ... there cannot have been many battlefields where there was such an accumulation of horrors within so small a compass.

About a fortnight later, between 5 and 7 February, Buller tried yet a third time to

Battle of Spion Kop, 24 January 1900

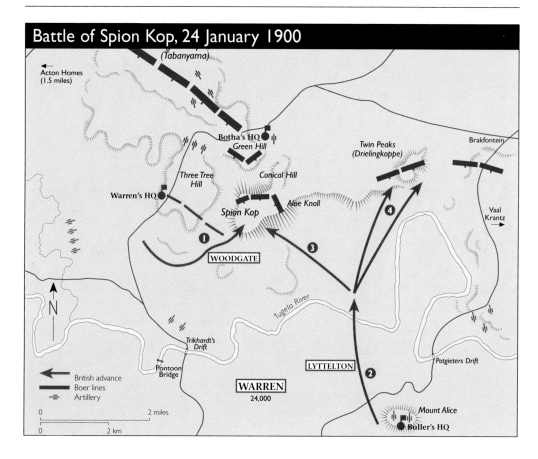

ABOVE
1. 9.00 pm, 23 January. Moving from Warren's camp, Woodgate's column attacks Spion Kop and takes it with ease. After efforts to entrench themselves they hold the position despite heavy rifle and artillery fire. Withdrawal begins around 8.00 pm on 24 January.
2. Morning, 24 January. Lyttleton advances after receiving a request for support from Warren.
3. Afternoon, 24 January. Lyttleton orders a rifle unit and mounted infantry to occupy the kop. On reaching the position the Rifles repulse a Boer attack then underway.
4. Afternoon, 24 January. While various units move against Spion Kop itself, another advances up the Twin Peaks. Ignoring a later order to retire, they seize the position from the Boers, thus puncturing a hole in their line. With no support forthcoming, their commander mortally wounded, and having received further instructions to withdraw, the Rifles do so with reluctance.

cross the Tugela and break through the hills. This time he confronted Boer forces occupying positions at Vaalkrans and Doornkop, two hills a few miles to the east, between Colenso and Spion Kop. Inadequate reconnaissance of the Boer positions on the

other side of the Tugela again hampered the British advance. Buller finally broke off the attack as the defending Johannesburg Commando stood firm, raining down destruction with their rifles and artillery, and inflicting a sharp, though minor, reverse.

OPPOSITE Besieging towns of strategic importance played an important part in the Boers' initial strategy. By rapid incursions into the Cape and Natal they sought to stun their opponents into negotiating a quick settlement before expected British reinforcements reversed the Boers' temporary numerical advantage. Mafeking, an important railway junction and administrative and supply center, was a natural target. Colonel Robert Baden-Powell, commanding the garrison, employed various ruses, including fake 'mine fields' and meaningless signal lights, to confound the besiegers, together with other tricks designed to exaggerate his strength. Relief finally came after 217 days, but little suffering occurred until the closing phase of the ordeal. In Britain news of the event led to great public rejoicing and propelled 'B-P' into the hallowed ranks of Victorian military heroes – one of the very few of the Boer War.

The siege of Mafeking

The besieged towns of Mafeking, Kimberley and Ladysmith played an important role in the conflict. Mafeking became the stuff of legends. Cronjé laid siege to the town with 8,000 men and 10 guns, including the famous siege gun known as 'Long Tom', a Creusot 94-pounder. The 42-year-old Colonel Robert Baden-Powell, future founder of the Boy Scout Movement, had about 1,000 men with which to defend the little town, together with four muzzle-loading cannon and a handful of machine-guns. With strict orders not to suffer heavy casualties, Cronjé held back at first, giving the resourceful and imaginative 'B-P' opportunities to prepare his defenses and inspire his garrison, which he did with a bizarre yet successful combination of amateur theatricals, amusing billboards and strict discipline. Morale remained high despite heavy rationing and continuous bombardment.

He did not hesitate to execute those blacks who stole food, and though he cut back the rations issued to the Africans, he also took the unprecedented step of arming them to bolster the size of the garrison. This incensed Cronjé, who sent Baden-Powell a message in the first month of the siege:

It is understood that you have armed Bastards, Fingos and Baralongs against us – in this you have committed an enormous act of wickedness ... reconsider this matter, even if it [should] cost you the loss of Mafeking ... disarm your blacks and thereby act the part of a white man in a white man's war.

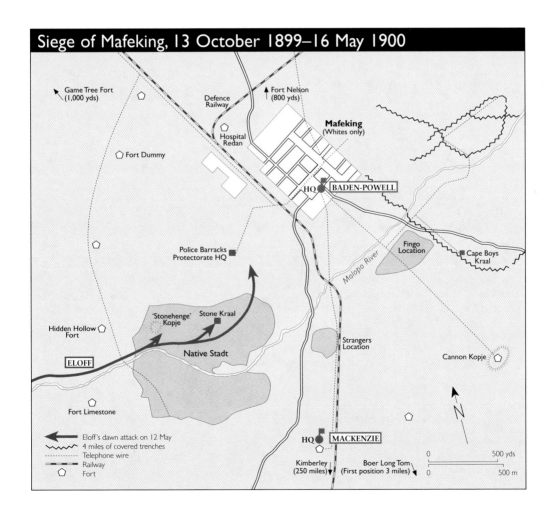

Siege of Mafeking, 13 October 1899–16 May 1900

Colonel Robert Baden-Powell, commander of the besieged garrison at Mafeking. 'B-P' devised every method he could not only to defend the town, but to entertain its inhabitants. He was one of the few British soldiers to emerge from the war with his reputation enhanced. (Ann Ronan Picture Library)

Baden-Powell had had the foresight before the siege to send away as large a proportion of the town's women and children as was possible, and ordered the construction of underground shell-proof shelters for those who remained. He encircled the town with earthworks and devised bogus 'mine fields',

simple wooden boxes which had wires connecting them to his headquarters. Most were filled with sand; others, containing dynamite, were detonated in public demonstrations intended to intimidate the besiegers and to mislead spies in the town. Above all, Baden-Powell remained resolute, the consummate leader of men:

All you have to do is to sit tight and when the time comes to shoot straight ... Take my word for it, if you act as I fully expect you to act, the Boers will never enter Mafeking.

Although the Boers bombarded Mafeking day and night, very little damage was actually done. Baden-Powell made light of the fact early in the siege by placing a satirical casualty list outside his headquarters, which read:

Killed: one hen
Wounded: one yellow dog
Smashed: one window

While the Boers' 'Long Tom' had more of a psychological than physical impact on the garrison, Baden-Powell felt that some response ought to be made to the incessant shelling. An 18th-century naval gun exhumed from a farmyard was restored to operation. When the initials 'BP' (representing the foundry of Bailey and Pegg) were found stamped on the barrel, the defenders hailed the discovery as a good omen, and promptly discovered, to their even greater joy, that the cannon, dubbed 'Lord Nelson', could send a roundshot bouncing nearly 3,000 yards, right into the midst of one of the Boers' encampments. The conversion and refurbishment of another half-buried cannon – loaded with home-made 18-pound shells, ultimately obliged the Boers to decamp almost 5 km (3 miles).

The Boer strategy of starving out the garrison imposed severe restrictions on food. As supplies dwindled many turned to feeding on locusts, available in abundance and prepared as a curry. Most residents survived on a porridge of ground oat husks. Nothing went to waste. Baden-Powell described how:

When a horse was killed, his mane and tail were cut off and sent to the hospital for stuffing mattresses and pillows. His shoes went to the foundry for making shells. His skin after having the hair scalded off, was boiled with his head and feet for many hours, chopped up small, and ... served out as 'brawn'.

His flesh was taken from the bones and minced in a great mincing machine and from his inside were made skins into which the meat was crammed and each man received a sausage as his ration. The bones were then boiled into rich

soup, which was dealt out at the different soup kitchens; and they were afterwards pounded into powder with which to adulterate the flour.

Such thrift and resourcefulness, allied to the inspiring leadership of Baden-Powell, sustained the besieged residents of Mafeking during their 217-day ordeal. British losses were low, though in the last days the Boers had made a final unsuccessful attempt to break in. The whole episode was cast as an epic of bravery and fortitude in the British press. The fact that many African workers had starved as a result of severe reductions in their rations was conveniently overlooked. The relief of the town was met with wild jubilation and Baden-Powell emerged as a national hero.

Roberts's offensive

Although there was no progress on the British drive towards Ladysmith, the arrival at Cape Town of Lord Roberts on 10 January 1900 brought new hope for operations on the western front where, by early February, Roberts, accompanied by his Chief of Staff, Major-General Lord Kitchener (1850–1916), commanded almost 37,000 men. The two men had long and colorful combat records and were well known to the British public, particularly Roberts, a distinguished veteran of the Indian Mutiny, the Abyssinian Expedition of 1867, and also the Second Afghan War.

Roberts intended to follow the original strategy of invading the Boer republics from the Cape Colony, making the relief of Kimberley his first objective. However, rather than try to dislodge the Boers from the ridge at Magersfontein, where they remained entrenched, he planned to use the western railway for as long as possible before marching round the Boers in a wide sweeping movement independent of the railway line. After retaking Kimberley, he then planned to abandon the railway and march east against first Bloemfontein, the capital of the Orange Free State, and then

Lord Roberts, Commander-in-Chief of British forces in South Africa, 1900–01. His appointment in the wake of 'Black Week' signaled a shift in British fortunes. Roberts achieved victory in the conventional phase of the war by taking both Boer capitals. (Ann Ronan Picture Library)

Pretoria, the capital of the Transvaal. Roberts intended to advance in one great undivided juggernaut, having learned from Buller's mistakes.

If the overall strategy remained largely the same, the tactics were to be different. Buller's and Methuen's unimaginative frontal attacks were to be replaced by encirclement, avoiding the sort of massive losses previously suffered in hopeless attacks against entrenched defenders. Roberts appreciated that such tactics would require a considerable body of mounted men, both

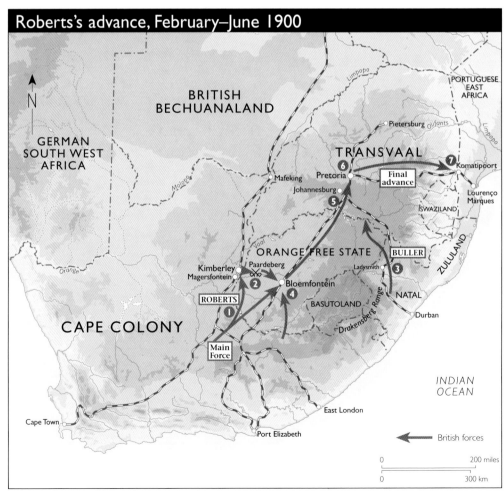

Roberts's advance, February–June 1900

Siege of Kimberley, 12 October 1899–15 February 1900

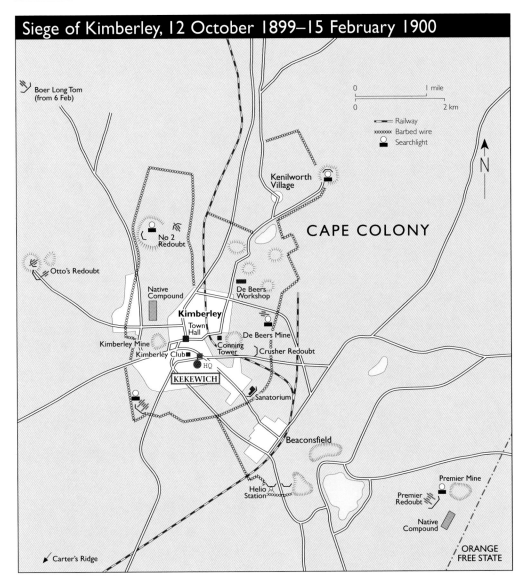

Boer Long Tom
(from 6 Feb)

0   1 mile
0   2 km

▬▬ Railway
xxxxxx Barbed wire
▪ Searchlight

Kenilworth
Village

CAPE COLONY

N

No 2
Redoubt

Otto's Redoubt

Native
Compound

De Beers
Workshop

Kimberley

Town
Hall

Kimberley Mine

De Beers Mine

Kimberley Club

Conning
Tower

Crusher Redoubt

HQ

KEKEWICH

Sanatorium

Beaconsfield

Premier Mine

Helio
Station

Premier
Redoubt

Native
Compound

**ORANGE
FREE STATE**

Carter's Ridge

OPPOSITE

1. 12 February. Roberts, with 37,000 men, begins march to Kimberley, abandoning use of the railway line in order to outflank his opponents. With a wide sweep around the main Boer positions near Magersfontein, Roberts's cavalry enters Kimberley on 15 February.

2. 18 February. Battle of Paardeberg. Abandoning his position at Magersfontein, Cronjé moves east towards Bloemfontein, crossing Roberts's line of advance before laagering at Paardeberg, where a direct British assault fails and suffers heavy casualties. Despite his tactical victory, Cronjé is surrounded and capitulates with over 4,000 men on 27 February.

3. 28 February. Buller, moving to relieve Ladysmith, engages the Boers in a series of clashes beginning on 14 February before liberating the town.

4. 13 March. Capture of Bloemfontein, capital of the Orange Free State.

5. 27 May. Roberts crosses the Vaal River at Vereeniging and occupies Johannesburg on the 31 May.

6. 5 June. Pretoria, capital of the Transvaal, falls to Roberts.

7. 24 September. Pole Carew reaches Komatipoort.

ABOVE Immediately after the outbreak of hostilities, Kimberley withstood a four-month siege by the Boers. The defenders, under Lieutenant-Colonel Kekewich, including 600 Regulars, 350 Cape police and 5,500 town volunteers, initially enjoyed adequate supplies of food and water and the defenses were considerably strengthened by the large quantities of firearms and ammunition provided by Cecil Rhodes and his company. The garrison launched two unsuccessful sorties in late November, but the defeat of Methuen's relief column at Magersfontein on 11 December obliged the garrison to sit tight and ration food while they endured sporadic artillery bombardment for another two months. British losses amounted to a mere 35 military and five civilian dead.

cavalry proper and mounted infantry. Major-General John French was therefore appointed to command a new division of 5,000 cavalry, and Roberts was sent more mounted infantry. The events of 'Black Week' had emphasized the urgent need for massive reinforcements to be dispatched to South Africa. By the time the campaign opened Roberts could muster about 50,000 troops, quite apart from Buller's force in Natal. Roberts concentrated a large force at Colesberg to distract the Boers in the south, in order to conceal his true purpose on the western front – to retake Kimberley and carry on against the rival capitals.

Setting out on 12 February, Roberts occupied Cronjé and De Wet with a division of infantry while his flying column of cavalry under French, moving at all possible speed, outflanked the Boers in a wide sweep

Cronjé surrendering to Roberts at Paardeberg, 27 February 1900. L. March Phillipps found the prisoners 'dressed in all sorts of ragged, motley-looking clothes… and it was a matter of some surprise, not to say disgust, to us to think that such a sorry crowd should be able to withstand disciplined troops in the way they did.' (Ann Ronan Picture Library)

through the Orange Free State. After a forced march French entered Kimberley on 15 February, ending the 124-day siege.

The remainder of the army followed behind, and although De Wet managed to capture a supply train crossing the Reit River, Roberts's advance had now threatened the Boer position at Magersfontein. Cronjé, entirely surprised by Roberts's abandonment of the railway lines as a means of advance, now found himself caught between the British and friendly territory. In grave risk of being entirely isolated from the republics, Cronjé was left with no choice but to abandon the area in favor of Bloemfontein, to the east. However, Cronjé's movement was seriously impaired by a substantial supply train and a large number of camp-followers. The course he took brought him within striking distance of Roberts's cavalry, which easily overtook him, forcing him to establish his laager at Paardeberg, on the north bank of the Modder River.

On 18 February, with Roberts ill, Lord Kitchener ordered his troops forward in a three-pronged frontal attack, supported by a

heavy artillery barrage. In the event, the British met the same tragic results as elsewhere: men pinned down under lethal fire, heavy losses and, finally, repulse. Kitchener lost 320 killed and 942 wounded – the largest loss in a single day during the entire war – as against the usual slight losses to the Boers. Nevertheless, the assault had inflicted such tremendous losses on Cronjé's horses and draft animals that he found himself unable to shift his wagon train to a less exposed position. Without their usual advantage of superior mobility, the Boers were left with no choice but to remain steadfast in their entrenchments and hope for the arrival of reinforcements.

The Boers were trapped, 40,000 British and Imperial troops and 100 guns managed to surround Cronjé's position and maintained a continuous and lethal bombardment with new, high-explosive lyddite shells. Despite Christiaan de Wet's attempts to relieve him, Cronjé found himself unable to break free. Fearful of an outbreak of disease as a result of such heavy losses both in men and animals, and with morale rapidly collapsing, Cronjé capitulated with his entire force of 4,105 men on 27 February – the anniversary of Majuba.

The event was devastating to the Boer cause, but it certainly did not spell the end of resistance elsewhere. On 7 March De Wet unsuccessfully attempted to hold back Roberts's advance at Poplar Grove, but British numbers were now telling. Three days later commandos under De la Rey engaged Roberts at Abrahamskraal, but made their escape as British troops sought to surround them. Roberts entered Bloemfontein on 13 March without firing a shot. The government of the Free State retreated quickly to Kroonstad.

British fortunes in Natal were also improving. White continued to hold out in Ladysmith which, since November, had been attacked only once by the Boers, unsuccessfully. With Roberts on the advance and Buller reinforced, he knew that relief was a matter of time if only he could resist the bombardment and repel any further assaults.

Buller now began a series of attacks which did much to recover his injured reputation and to reverse the tide of the war. In early February he began to probe the Boer defenses along the Tugela, before, on 17 February, finally launching a number of well-coordinated attacks against a series of ridges and kopjes south of the river, deploying his men in open order with close artillery support. By 18 February the Boers had been driven across the river, and Buller prepared to cross it and face the Boer entrenchments which lined the series of hills ahead – Wynne's Hill, Pieter's Hill, Hart's Hill and Railway Hill.

Assisted in their progress by a creeping artillery barrage, Buller's men crossed the Tugela on 22 February. The Boers put up their usual dogged defense, but the British carried on undaunted and managed to outflank their opponents. On the fifth day of the battle the British broke through the last strongpoint, at Pieter's Hill. Private Tucker recounted how 'we all gave a good, hearty cheer and yells of 'Remember Majuba!' and we started off on the race for the top of the hill.' The Boer lines collapsed, forcing them to make a hasty retreat to the Biggarsberg and Drakensberg.

Buller did not pursue, content instead to relieve the garrison at Ladysmith, which his cavalry entered on 28 February and prompting White's celebrated declaration: 'Thank God we kept the flag flying.' Private Tucker received a subdued welcome: 'Instead of being cheered by all as we had imagined, most of them seemed to say with their looks: "Well, you have come at last, but you have taken your time over it."' The siege had lasted for 118 days, with 170 killed in the fighting around the town and 393 civilian and military dead through disease, mostly typhoid fever. All told, Buller's losses in the campaign – about 5,000 men – accounted for a sixth of his total force. The Boers lost perhaps 400–500 men – also a heavy proportional loss. Roberts's offensive had met with success on every front. While the British rested the Boers began to reorganize their dispersed men and assess their declining fortunes.

Close-quarter fighting on Hlangwane. To break through to Ladysmith, Buller had to outflank the Boer trench lines defending Colenso, particularly those on Hlangwane, a strategically important hill north-east of the town. On 19 February 1900 British troops successfully stormed it, and having established heavy guns on its summit, rendered Colenso untenable. (Ann Ronan Picture Library)

The British successes achieved in February 1900 clearly demonstrated that the tide had turned. The Boer offensives into the Cape and Natal had been thwarted and thrown back, and Roberts's inexorable advance had carried him into the Orange Free State.

The war now entered a quiet phase as Roberts rested, resupplied and reorganized at Bloemfontein for the next seven weeks. To the British, at least, the war appeared to be winding down. The fall of Pretoria, capital of the Transvaal, was the next obvious objective and the apparent key to victory. The Boers, for their part, held a joint council of the two republics at Kroonstad on 17 March, at which they decided to abandon the use of wagon laagers. They hoped this would increase their mobility and it ultimately proved a sound policy, freeing the Boers from their cumbersome supply trains and enabling them to elude the numerous and slower British forces when necessary.

By this time the republics had produced a number of charismatic, energetic and bold leaders such as Christiaan de Wet, Louis Botha and Koos de la Rey. On the death of Joubert on 27 March, Botha succeeded as chief of the Transvaal forces. It was De Wet, however, the new Chief-Commandant of Free State forces, who emerged as the champion of the new mobility. Indeed, for the remainder of the war De Wet would harass British infantry and supply columns – particularly those that Roberts had dispersed throughout the southern Free State in an effort to suppress further resistance. Suddenly appearing in the rear of British formations, De Wet's highly mobile commandos would make lightning attacks and then disappear off into the veld. Having been granted a short leave of absence by De Wet, a benefit of the lull in the fighting, large numbers of Free State burghers reassembled at the Sand River on 25 March, ready to strike back.

De Wet soon achieved one of his greatest successes of the war when, on 31 March, he attacked the Bloemfontein water works at Sannah's Post (Sannaspos), 30 km (19 miles) east of the capital. There, Piet De Wet (1861–1929), younger brother of Christiaan, scared off the British garrison, about a

General Christiaan De Wet. Although he served throughout the war, De Wet is most closely associated with the guerrilla phase, when he carried out numerous raids and managed to evade capture despite the considerable efforts made by Kitchener to trap him against blockhouse lines. (Ann Ronan Picture Library)

thousand men under Brigadier-General Robert Broadwood (1862–1917), who when fired upon obligingly withdrew for the apparent safety of Bloemfontein, becoming caught in an ambush by Christiaan de Wet, with 350 men, at Koornspruitdrift. At a cost of 13 killed and wounded, the Boers inflicted 159 casualties on Broadwood's force and captured 373 men, seven guns, 116 wagons and a large amount of ammunition. The Boers retained possession of the waterworks long enough to cause a severe water shortage in Bloemfontein, leading to an acute outbreak of typhoid there which hospitalized many of Roberts's men. Amidst heavy rain on 4 April, De Wet also captured 450 British troops at Mostertshoek, near Reddersburg.

Notwithstanding these various minor setbacks, the British continued to enjoy

general success, in particular the relief of Mafeking on 17 May. While British troops were liberating that town, Roberts's 100,000 troops, marching north on both sides of the railway line, started their advance on Pretoria, beginning on 3 May. To oppose him Botha, who had left the front in Natal and had no more than 8,000 burghers at his disposal, joined with De Wet to try to block Roberts at the Sand River. Again the British attempted to encircle the Boers rather than confront them directly. On 10 May Botha discovered French sweeping round his right flank, leaving the Boers no option but to withdraw. As he took the main points on the railway line between Bloemfontein and Pretoria, Roberts appeared unstoppable. The annexation of the Free State as the Orange River Colony on 24 May served to highlight the success of the British campaign.

On 27 May Roberts crossed the frontier into the Transvaal. Ian Hamilton, now promoted to lieutenant-general for his services at Ladysmith, encountered a Boer force under De la Rey on 29 May at Doornkop, where he lost heavily. Still, Roberts's main force carried on unopposed, taking the Witwatersrand goldmines and entering Johannesburg on 30 May. On 2 June Kruger and his government left Pretoria and proceeded eastwards along the Delagoa Bay railway as far as Machadodorp. Roberts entered Pretoria unopposed three days later. The Transvaal, it seemed, had been all but knocked out of the war.

At the same time, Buller continued his slow advance through Natal, engaging the Boers in the passes of the Drakensberg Range before, on 12 June, passing the frontier into the Transvaal. On the following day came the last encounters between Roberts's troops and the commandos withdrawing eastwards towards Portuguese East Africa. With the Boers in retreat practically everywhere, it seemed the war was nearly at an end. Indeed, on 31 May Kruger and Botha had telegraphed their opposites in the Free State Government to point out the futility of further resistance. Yet as far as Steyn and De Wet were concerned the war was not lost. One option remained to be exploited: guerrilla warfare. Thus, the conflict entered a period of transition between conventional fighting and the hit-and-run tactics already employed by De Wet. L. March Phillipps summed up the irony of the situation:

It is generally considered rather a coup in war, I believe, to take the enemy's capital, isn't it? Like taking a queen in chess. We keep on taking capitals, but I can't see it seems to make much difference. The Boers set no store by them apparently; neither Bloemfontein nor Pretoria have been seriously defended, and they go on fighting after their loss just as if nothing had happened.

The guerrilla phase

The fall of Bloemfontein and Pretoria did not bring the war to an end, as Roberts initially believed. On the contrary, the war merely entered a new phase that was to last another two years. Indeed, evidence of the Boers' willingness to carry on the struggle quickly became obvious to Roberts, who appreciated that large areas in both republics remained beyond British control. In particular, his line of communication through the Orange Free State was inadequately defended and open to attack at numerous points. Notwithstanding the loss of their capitals the Boers enjoyed some advantages. Those leaders who remained in the field were largely young, determined and imaginative and, no longer obliged to defend the capitals, they could deploy the remaining commandos as guerrillas.

By this time there were perhaps only 25,000 Boers still offering resistance, but they were well mounted and elusive, with up to 400,000 sq km (about 150,000 square miles) in which to operate. The Boers, moreover, understood the terrain far better than their adversaries, who continued to rely on the railway lines and larger towns for their supplies. The countryside could not be completely controlled, a fact which left the

British with an apparently insoluble problem, and one that would be faced on many future occasions by modern and sophisticated armies later in the 20th century.

Roberts made an early and concerted effort to quash the guerrilla movement. First, he issued proclamations on 31 May and 1 June, meant to persuade the burghers still in the field to hand in their weapons. Next, on 16 June he followed this up with a new, more drastic decree: if the Boers struck railway and telegraph lines and stations, homes and farms in the area of these attacks would be put to the torch. Such forms of retaliation had been practiced on an ad hoc basis since the beginning of the year: now Roberts made the policy official, providing a legal precedent for the more comprehensive 'scorched earth' policy to be applied by Kitchener in the following year.

In the field itself, Roberts opened an offensive intended to drive the Free State forces eastwards in order to trap them against the Basutoland border in a pincer movement during June and July 1900 in what became known as the 'first De Wet hunt.' He took Bethlehem on 7 July and compelled the Free State forces to take refuge behind the Witteberg Range. De Wet and Steyn, with 2,000 men and the Free State Government, managed to elude forces under Lieutenant-General Sir Archibald Hunter (1856–1936), but Marthinus Prinsloo was forced to surrender about 4,400 men, half the remaining Free State forces, on 30 July.

De Wet, meanwhile, showed himself a master of maneuver and deception, easily outwitting his pursuers as he escaped across the border into the Transvaal, despite the fact that as many as 50,000 troops in converging columns sought to destroy him. Free State commandos all the while struck with considerable success against the railway lines, notably the line linking Potchefstroom and Krugersdorf. Superior scouting, firm discipline and excellent mobility served De Wet extremely well, and he was also assisted by defects in British communications and intelligence-gathering.

De Wet was, nevertheless, nearly caught by approaching British columns in an encirclement at Magaliesberg. He managed to escape across the mountains with his tiny force of 250 burghers in one of many daring escapes. As a result of this first De Wet hunt, Roberts's advance along the Delagoa railway was delayed for weeks while time and energy were devoted elsewhere to capturing De Wet.

Meanwhile, in the north-east, Botha was busy attempting to stem the British advance towards the Portuguese East Africa border, where Kruger had established his government in exile. The Boers could not resist for long, however. On 27 August combined forces under Roberts and Buller pierced their defenses at Bergendal and reached the frontier at Komatipoort, forcing Kruger to board a Dutch warship and go into exile on 11 September. Both republics had, in any event, decided to send Kruger to Europe to seek assistance from the major powers in an effort not only to achieve peace, but also to preserve the independence of the Boer republics. In Kruger's absence Schalk Burger was appointed as acting-president of the Transvaal, notwithstanding the fact that, by this time, both republics had been proclaimed British colonies.

The conventional phase of the war was not quite over. On 11 June Roberts attacked Botha's line of defense 30 km (18 miles) east of Pretoria. The following day Hamilton pierced the Boer lines at Diamond Hill, near Donkerhoek, but Botha disappeared in the darkness, falling back east in order to protect his rear from Buller's columns approaching from Natal. When it was clear by the end of July that the first De Wet hunt had failed, Roberts turned eastwards to confront Botha. On 15 August Roberts and Buller joined up their troops at Ermelo, bringing the combined British force to 20,000, ready to oppose Botha's 5,000. Between 21 and 27 August the two sides fought a sharp action at Bergendal, where Roberts's artillery obliged Botha to retreat towards Lydenburg. A few days later, on 1 September, British authorities formally declared the Transvaal a Crown colony. With the arrival of British troops at Komatipoort on the border with Portuguese East Africa, Roberts theoretically controlled all of the Transvaal south of the Delagoa railway line. Yet this appearance of control was misleading. Beyond the garrison towns, outside the immediate reach of his troops, the commandos still roamed, and when British troops left an area, Boer authorities simply reinstated themselves.

Anxious to encourage large numbers of disaffected Cape Afrikaners to flock to the republican cause, De Wet invaded the Cape Colony in November, forcing Roberts to divert troops from the Free State and Transvaal. Moving south with 1,500 men, De Wet captured the British garrison of 400 men at Dewetsdorp on 23 November, prompting the 'second De Wet hunt', involving General Knox, with three flying columns and thousands of other troops sent by rail from the Transvaal. De Wet's operations in December proved disappointing, as heavy rains impeded movement. Nevertheless, he managed to elude his pursuers, most notably in a breakthrough at Sprinkannsnek, assisted by Commandant Gideon Scheepers (1878–1902), a Cape rebel who was later captured and executed by the British for murder, arson and the ill-treatment of prisoners.

Employing both speed and surprise, even greater success was achieved when on the morning of 13 December at Nooitgedacht, 1,500 men under Major-General Ralph Clements were surprised at a cliff's edge on the slopes of the Magaliesberg by Boer forces under Assistant Commandant-General Christiaan Beyers (1869–1914), De la Rey and the newly appointed Jan Smuts (1870–1950), a distinguished Transvaal attorney destined to become one of the greatest Boer leaders. At a cost of 78 of their own men, the Boers inflicted over 300 casualties, took about the same number of prisoners, as well as a substantial quantity of provisions, weapons, ammunition and draft animals. The victory at Nooitgedacht reinvigorated the Boer cause: the guerrilla war was now well underway. As the year closed, Vecht-General Ben Viljoen (1868–1917) captured the British garrison at

Boers surprising a British camp. During the guerrilla phase of the war, particularly in the last months, the Boers used raids on small outposts and garrison towns as a means of replenishing their stocks of food, clothing, and ammunition. (Ann Ronan Picture Library)

Helvetia in a night attack on 28–29 December. In the same month Roberts, keen to take up his new post as Commander-in-Chief of the army in succession to Lord Wolseley, left for Britain in December 1900 and passed supreme command of forces in South Africa to his Chief of Staff, Lord Kitchener, who had 210,000 troops available to him.

Kitchener's offensive: the final phase

Kitchener inaugurated a new, bitter phase in the conflict, meant to wear down the Boers through attrition. His strategy contained three elements: scorched earth, internment and containment. Roberts had recognized that a systematic, methodical approach to the guerrilla problem had to be adopted. As early as June 1900 he had ordered the burning of farms known to be the property of Boers still on commando. Finding himself unable to capture or eliminate the various

LEFT Lord Kitchener. Victor of the Battle of Omdurman over the Dervishes in 1898, he succeeded Roberts as Commander-in-Chief in South Africa. Kitchener is best remembered for the ruthless measures he employed to defeat the Boers during the guerrilla phase of the war. (Ann Ronan Picture Library)

guerrilla forces, he had implemented a straightforward, yet brutal policy: destruction of their means of supply. Kitchener now continued this process, though on a much larger scale, employing a full-scale scorched earth policy intended to lay waste to all Boer farmsteads within the reach of his forces. Both republics experienced wholesale devastation, with entire towns and thousands of farmsteads set aflame or otherwise rendered uninhabitable. The destruction of supplies of food, both in storage and still in the fields or pastures, was also paramount in a strategy meant to deprive the commandos of sustenance,

BELOW A defiant Boer women stands before her farmhouse as British troops set it alight. General Kelly-Kenny, for one, issued uncompromising orders: '... they [women and children] have forfeited all right to consideration and must now suffer for their persistently ignoring warnings against harbouring and assisting our enemy ...'. (Ann Ronan Picture Library)

intelligence and temporary abodes. Livestock were slaughtered or seized in their tens of thousands, and fields once containing grain were laid waste by fire.

The second strand of Kitchener's strategy involved internment on a massive scale. Boer non-combatants – almost exclusively women, children and old people – deprived of their livelihoods, could not be abandoned to wander in the open, and exposed to the elements. The British solution, ostensibly humanitarian, was simple and brutal.

Thousands were loaded onto wagons and moved to makeshift refugee camps, later known as concentration camps. The Spanish had first introduced such camps a few years earlier during their struggle against Cuban guerrillas. These British concentration camps

Boers attacking a blockhouse. Deprived of their artillery by the later stages of the war, the Boers found blockhouses almost impregnable. Note the tin cans festooned on the barbed wire: a rudimentary yet effective method of raising the alarm when attackers sought to climb over. (Ann Ronan Picture Library)

were unsanitary, short of food and overcrowded: ideal conditions in which disease and malnutrition could prey on the unfortunate internees.

Kitchener's policy of containment, combined with great 'drives' – some over 80 km (50 miles) long – constituted the third element of his strategy to cope with the guerrillas and finish the war. He understood that he could not catch or destroy the remaining commandos without placing strict limits on their freedom of movement before sweeping them from the veld. This policy was not as clinical in practice as it sounded in theory. The sweeps were often accompanied by looting, as well as destruction. Phillipps recorded that the British soldier sometimes regarded it almost as sport:

Looting ... is one of his perpetual joys. Not merely looting for profit ... but looting for the sheer fun of the destruction; tearing down pictures to kick their boots through them; smashing furniture for the fun of smashing it, and maybe dressing up in women's clothes to finish with, and dancing among the ruins they have made. To pick up a good heavy stone and send it wallop right through the works of a piano is a great moment for Tommy.

Kitchener, however, believed that ideally such sweeps would drive the Boers – not unlike a gigantic pheasant hunt – before him, trapping them against lines of blockhouses and barbed wire. Roberts had first ordered the construction of blockhouses in March 1900 in order to protect the Cape Town–Bloemfontein railway, on which he relied for his supplies. But defending vulnerable targets like railways, roads and towns was not enough: the guerrillas' freedom of movement had now to be impeded as much as possible. Blockhouses, initially rectangular and built of stone, were ultimately round and made of corrugated iron and earth, covered with strong tin roofs, protected by trenches and barbed wire. Strong enough to withstand rifle fire, once erected in sufficient numbers and linked by thousands of miles of barbed wire fencing,

they became an elaborate network spanning wide areas of the former Boer republics. By the end of the war, blockhouse chains extended for 6,000 km (3,700 miles) and effectively hampered the previously unrestricted movements of the commandos.

Kitchener's first large-scale drive opened on 28 January 1901, involving seven columns, in total 14,000 men and 58 guns, moving through the Transvaal between the Delagoa and Natal railway lines. Facing vastly superior numbers, most of the commandos fell back without a fight and managed to break through the lines, behind which they were largely safe. Nonetheless, there they found large areas totally devastated, making subsistence in the field extremely difficult. By the time Kitchener's forces eventually reached the Natal border in mid-April, they had swept the veld clean of civilians and had laid waste to the landscape. They had, however, made scarcely any impact on the commandos. Only a handful, known as 'hands-uppers', had voluntarily surrendered to the British. Some went so far as to change sides – the 'joiners' – while those who doggedly remained on commando came to be known as 'bitter-enders'. Kitchener's radical approach to the guerrilla problem proved counterproductive, at least at the outset, for it hardened the resolve of the bitter-enders to carry on in spite of the sufferings of Boer civilians, and released them from the responsibility of having to protect their properties and loved ones.

NEXT PAGE Roberts began construction of blockhouses in March 1900 to protect vulnerable railway lines on which British forces relied for their supply. Blockhouses were originally built of stone, but cost and the slow rate of construction led to their replacement by layers of corrugated iron packed with earth between them. During the guerrilla phase of the war the system expanded to include chains of blockhouses meant to impede the Boers' movement as well as to protect railways. These could be built in a day, protected by trenches and barbed wire, and manned by as few as seven men. Nearly 8,000 blockhouses were erected, requiring over 50,000 men to garrison them. They were proof against small arms fire, often linked to one another by wire, and covered about 3,700 miles. Blockhouses proved an effective means of impeding movement and played an important part in ultimate victory.

Blockhouse system, June 1901–May 1902

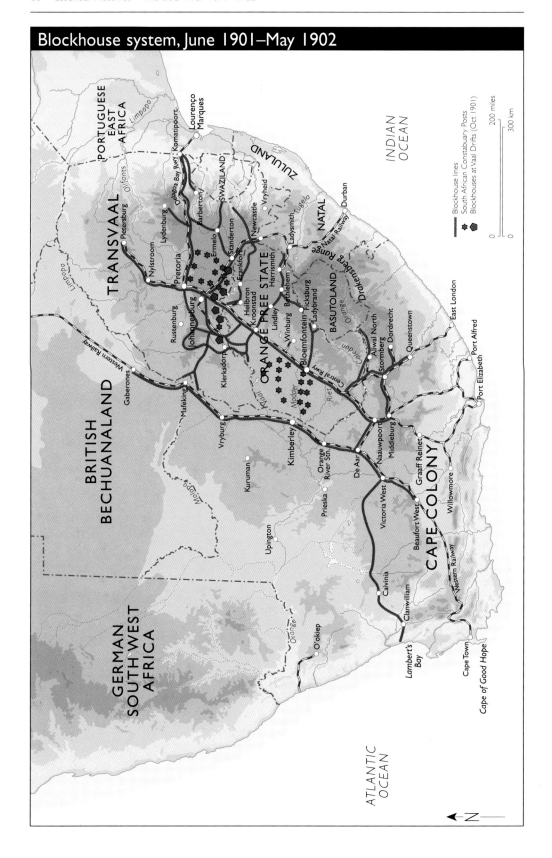

Smuts's invasion of Cape Colony, September 1901–May 1902

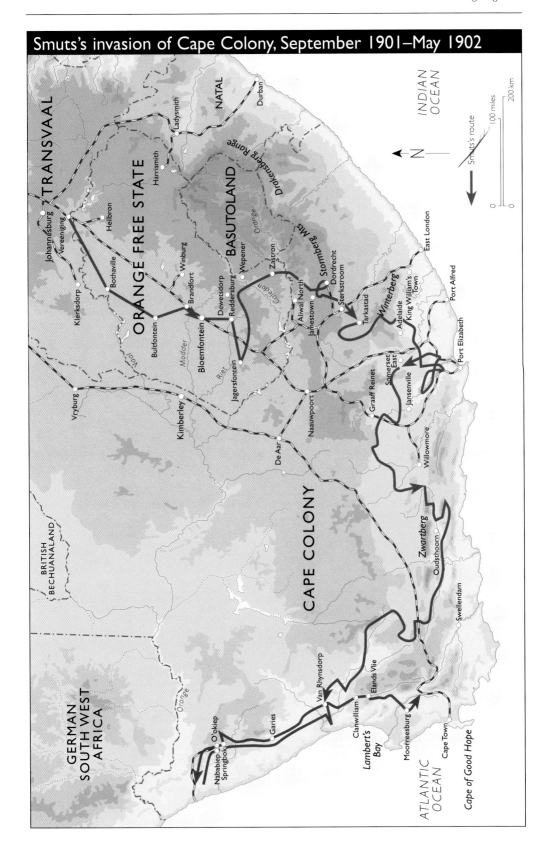

PREVIOUS PAGE Hoping to cause chaos and recruit rebel Afrikaners to the Boer cause, Jan Smuts boldly led a token force of 250 men across the Orange River to bring the war directly to the largely untouched and predominantly loyal Cape Colony. Before him lay a vast area where Smuts knew the authorities would not take reprisals against the inhabitants for any suspected collaboration, as was standard practice in the Orange Free State and the Transvaal. Although harried throughout his raid, Smuts obliged the British to impose martial law and caused considerable mayhem across the entire length of the colony.

At the same time as Kitchener was executing his drive through the Transvaal, De Wet launched his second invasion of the Cape. Kitchener sent 14,000 troops by rail and road in over a dozen flying columns against a Boer force of 3,000 in the 'third De Wet hunt.' But De Wet's hit-and-run tactics kept the British confused as to his location and direction of movement. He still managed to sever lines of communication, strike at convoys and tear up railway lines, to the great consternation of his opponents. He then escaped across the Orange River near Philippolis on 10 February, finally reaching the Free State on 28 February – but not before his men and horses had suffered badly from privation and fatigue. Worse still, this second invasion had totally failed in its objectives. De Wet's men were quite exhausted, and Cape Afrikaners had not joined his force in large numbers. De Wet would, hereafter, remain on the defensive, though others, such as Assistant Chief-Commandant P. H. Kritzinger (1870–1935), another effective guerrilla leader, led their own forays. Having met with considerable success after crossing into the Cape Colony in December 1900, he conducted a second raid in May 1901 and later a third, which ended in his capture. During his operations Kritzinger had ruthlessly executed any blacks found working for the British. Though he was put on trial for murder, he was subsequently acquitted.

Meanwhile, abortive peace talks took place at Middelburg in late February, but with their failure the war continued. Kitchener now applied his scorched earth policy more intensively than ever and over

an increasingly wide area, leaving those Boers still on the veld during the winter (June–August) of 1901 critically short of food and shelter. The commandos began to operate less frequently, women and children often chose to live exposed on the veld rather than face internment, and Boer forces were obliged to make up for shortages of food, weapons, ammunition and clothing by seizing them from small British detachments at isolated posts. Some measures smacked of even greater desperation: without facilities for holding prisoners of war, the Boers had no option but to release their captives as soon as they were taken.

Acting-president Burger and other members of the Transvaal Government began to lose heart. President Steyn of the Free State, on the other hand, together with De Wet and De la Rey, urged resistance to the last man when on 20 June they all gathered at Waterval. Steyn, De Wet and De la Rey eventually convinced Burger to hold firm. The Boer leaders planned a new invasion of the Cape Colony to try to divert Kitchener's attention away from his drives to the north. Kitchener in the meantime issued a proclamation on 7 August, demanding that Boer officers surrender their firearms by 15 September or suffer banishment from South Africa and the confiscation of their property. In the event, few burghers laid down their arms. Indeed, Smuts's invasion of the Cape in September graphically demonstrated that several thousand bitter-enders remained at large.

First moving into the eastern Cape almost as far as Port Elizabeth on the coast, Smuts then turned west and proceeded into the south-eastern districts before heading north and north-west, where he linked up with other commandos and took several towns near O'Okiep in April 1902. Cape authorities imposed martial law, seized livestock from rebel farms and rounded up those suspected of collaboration. In the course of the war about 13,000 Cape rebels – about 10 percent of the white population – joined the Boer cause, and somewhat more volunteered to serve on the British side either as police or mounted troops. Many other Cape Afrikaners who did not themselves take up arms, did offer some assistance to Smuts's men and other raiders, to whom they were bound by common culture and language.

Kitchener, taking advantage of the now extensive network of blockhouses and lines of barbed wire, now began his 'new model drives' – huge sweeps involving multiple columns sometimes extending 80 km (50 miles) in length. With 30,000 men at his disposal, along with armored trains, he made three attempts in February and March 1902 to corner De Wet against the blockhouse lines that crisscrossed the north-eastern section of the Orange Free State. While this strategy trapped relatively few Boers, in general Kitchener's drives of this period proved successful. Boer morale suffered under the continuous pressure exerted by the relentless pursuit, and British troops

General Koos de la Rey, a versatile leader who enjoyed success in both the conventional and guerrilla phases of the war, as at Graspan, the Modder River, Nooitgedacht, and Tweesbosch. A wound prevented him from fighting at Magersfontein, but his suggestion that trenches be dug in front of the hills rather than on top clinched victory for Cronjé. (Ann Ronan Picture Library)

Boers charging Lieutenant-Colonel Gough's mounted infantry at Blood River Poort, 17 September 1901. Five hundred of Botha's men struck the British flank, capturing Gough and 241 officers and men, and inflicting 44 other casualties. (Ann Ronan Picture Library)

systematically destroyed stocks of food as they advanced across a broad front.

At about the same time, in the western Transvaal, Lord Methuen was continuing his hunt for De la Rey, who found his freedom of movement seriously restricted by the ubiquitous blockhouse lines. Other problems now dogged the remaining Boer units, many of which were operating with fewer than 200 men. Food, clothing and ammunition were growing increasingly scarce; winter was approaching; the numbers of 'joiners'

actually assisting the British in seeking out their own compatriots was on the rise; and losses, through death and capture, could not easily be replaced.

Two final battles took place prior to the conclusion of hostilities: Tweebosch, fought beside the Little Hart River on 7 March, and Roodewal, near the Harts River, on 11 April. In the former action, which proved to be De la Rey's finest achievement, his burghers struck Methuen's rearguard, inflicting almost 200 casualties and taking 850 prisoners – including the wounded Methuen himself – at a cost of 34 to himself. At Roodewal, a Boer attack led by General Kemp was repulsed by a combined British force, which killed nearly 50 of De la Rey's men and wounded 120.

Deneys Reitz

Several days before the outbreak of the war, Deneys Reitz (1882–1944), aged just 17, left on commando. He was to remain in the field until the last day of the conflict. Immediately after the war, he committed to paper his adventures, exploits, hardships, combat experiences and harrowing escapes which would later be published in 1929 as *Commando: A Boer Journal of the Boer War*, a minor military classic. The accuracy of his account – unromanticized and refreshingly free from both bitterness and bravado – was authenticated by many of those who shared his experiences, which at times have a storybook quality. Reitz describes in compelling detail his trials and triumphs with the Pretoria Commando, from the first action of the Natal campaign under Botha at Talana, to the siege of Ladysmith and the bloody affair at Spion Kop, through the guerrilla phase of the war in the western Transvaal under De la Rey, and on to the final stages when he accompanied Smuts on his daring incursion into the Cape Colony in 1901. Reitz was also present with Smuts at the signing of the Treaty of Vereeniging.

Reitz witnessed all the horrors of the war, watching as his comrades were killed in combat or executed for wearing captured British uniforms. He himself suffered the considerable hardships of the conflict, including a shortage of food and exposure to the severe climate. His account of the fighting just prior to the investment of Ladysmith provides an accurate impression of combat conditions during much of the conventional phase of the war.

The son of the Transvaal State Secretary, Reitz was well educated, intelligent, keen for the fray and innocent of the true nature of war. Though privileged by the standards of Boer society, he was by no means pampered:

[We] ... learned to ride, shoot, and swim almost as soon as we could walk, and there was a string of hardy Basuto ponies in the stables, on which we were often away for weeks at a time, riding over the game-covered plains by day, and sleeping under the stars at night, hunting, fishing and camping to our heart's content ...

Having personally received his Mauser rifle from President Kruger, Reitz and the rest of the Pretoria Commando of about 300 men left by train to the Natal border just before the outbreak of war. At dawn on the morning after the declaration of war, the assembled commandos set out. 'As far as the eye could see,' Reitz recalled, 'the plain was alive with horsemen, guns, and cattle, all steadily going forward to the frontier. The scene was a stirring one, and I shall never forget riding to war with that great host.' Still, in the field, Reitz's commando possessed only five days' ration of biltong (dried meat), and were exposed to the elements. 'It was our first introduction to the real hardships of war, and our martial feelings were considerably damped by the time the downpour ceased at daybreak.'

At Talana, Reitz encountered the British for the first time, amidst a furious exchange of artillery. 'We could see nothing, but heavy fighting had started close by, for the roar of the guns increased and at times we heard the rattle of small arms and Maxims.' As Reitz and the other members of his unit approached the scene, they discovered a party of British soldiers, 'Khakis', taking refuge in a small farmhouse and manning the stone walls of a cattle kraal. The place was soon surrounded. Reitz made for the dry bed of a stream in front of the British position, which put him in the line of fire:

... now, for the first time in my life, I heard the sharp hiss of rifle-bullets about my ears, and

for the first time I experienced the thrill of riding into action. My previous ideas of a battle had been different, for there was almost nothing to see here. The soldiers were hidden, and, except for an occasional helmet and the spurts of dust flicked up around us, there was nothing.

A sharp exchange of rifle fire followed, but when the Boers brought up a Creusot gun and opened fire, the British raised a white flag and threw down their arms.

Reitz soon lost his preconceived notions of a glamorous war. He had already discovered that his adversaries remained largely unseen in battle. This added a particularly frightening new element to warfare, the 'empty' battlefield experience so characteristic of First World War memoirs.

It was, understandably, the sight of the dead that made the greatest impression:

These were the first men I had seen killed in anger, and their ashen faces and staring eyeballs came as a great shock, for I had pictured the dignity of death in battle, but I now saw that it was horrible to look upon.

After Talana, General White ordered a withdrawal towards Ladysmith, which he reached on 26 October, his troops having exhausted themselves during long marches in searing heat, which alternated with bitterly cold nights. The Boers followed, and Reitz took part in the actions around Ladysmith, where his commando established itself on the slopes overlooking the town, building earthworks in case of a British sortie.

White understood that to avoid being bottled up in Ladysmith he must assume the offensive. On 30 October British troops advanced in an attempt to drive the Boers from their makeshift defenses on a number of eminences surrounding the town, including Pepworth Hill and Nicholson's Nek, at both of which Reitz was present. At dawn the Boers on Pepworth Hill began to rain down artillery fire on the attackers:

... what with the thunder of the British guns and of our own, the crash of bursting shells and the din of a thousand rifles, there was a volume of sound unheard in South Africa before. I was awed rather than frightened, and, once I had got over my first impression, I felt excited by all I saw and keenly joined in the firing. We were so successful that by the time the foremost infantrymen came within 1,200 yards of us, many fallen dotted the veld, and their advance wavered before the hail of bullets.

With the British attack frustrated, Reitz went in search of his brother, making his way to the top of Nicholson's Nek, a broad, flat-topped hill strewn with boulders and brush, occupied by Free State burghers. His

Boers in action. This simple photograph reveals two distinguishing characteristics of the war: the complete absence of uniformity in Boer dress, and the scarcity of natural cover in the bleak South African landscape. (Ann Ronan Picture Library)

enemy was, once again, unseen. In fact, the British were only 27 to 37 m (30 to 40 yards) away, posted behind rocks and any other available shelter. Here Reitz began to appreciate that the British were no match for his comrades in a sharpshooting contest:

Time after time I saw [British] soldiers looking over their defences to fire, and time after time I heard the thud of a bullet finding its mark, and could see the unfortunate man fall back out of sight, killed or wounded.

As Reitz and the others moved to occupy the abandoned ground they surveyed the field, strewn with the large number of casualties they had inflicted. Finally, around noon, the shrill of a bugle, carrying above the sound of rifle fire, signaled, together with a white flag held aloft, the surrender of over a thousand British soldiers. 'Hundreds of khaki-clad figures rose from among the rocks and walked towards us, their rifles at the trail.'

A short time later Reitz watched as many more thousands of British troops that had assembled on the plain in front of Ladysmith that morning were now in full retreat into the town itself, throwing up 'great clouds of dust,' a withdrawal that 'had every appearance of a rout.' The elation Reitz felt about the victory was tempered by the sickening sights of the aftermath of battle:

Dead and wounded soldiers lay all around, and the cries and groans of agony, and the dreadful sights, haunted me for many a day, for though I had seen death by violence of late, there had been nothing to approach the horrors accumulated here.

The day subsequently became known to the British as 'Mournful Monday'. Their defeat in front of, and refuge in, Ladysmith, would leave them trapped for the next 118 days, rendering White's field force of almost 10,000 troops useless.

For Reitz, the success at Ladysmith provided only temporary satisfaction. General Joubert refused to exploit the opportunity to rush the town and drive the British out. The Boers could not know that the siege would

bring a premature end to the Boer offensive and sow the seeds of ultimate defeat:

There was not a man who did not believe we were heading straight for the coast, and it was as well that the future was hidden from us, and that we did not know how strength and enthusiasm were to be frittered away in a meaningless siege, and in the holding of useless positions, when our only salvation lay in rapid advance.

At the end of the war Reitz refused to sign the oath of allegiance and promptly settled in Madagascar, where he nearly died of malaria. In 1906 he was persuaded by friends to return, and later took part in suppressing the Boer rebellion of 1914. He went on to serve under Jan Smuts in the campaign in German West Africa and later against the Germans in East Africa. He was promoted to colonel of his mounted regiment and, later in the war, went to France, where – the process of reconciliation having run full course – he enlisted in the British Army and commanded the 1st Royal Scots Fusiliers. He was wounded twice, the second time severely, in early 1918, but recovered to fight in the closing phases of the war on the Western Front.

After the war Reitz returned to South Africa. He served in the cabinet under Smuts, his former commander, and as Deputy Prime Minister in 1939. Shortly before he died in 1944, Reitz, then an extremely popular High Commissioner for South Africa in London, received an unexpected visitor. Into his office strolled a man smiling, bearing a long, slender parcel wrapped in brown paper. 'We have actually met before, Colonel,' the mysterious visitor explained, 'but under rather less auspicious circumstances. Perhaps you will recognize this.' He unwrapped the parcel, which contained a Mauser. This was the very rifle which, its magazine emptied, Reitz had abandoned on the battlefield more than 40 years earlier. It was the same weapon with which Reitz had shot the man standing before him, Lord Vivian. Speechless, Reitz looked down to discover his own name carved on the rifle butt.

Imperial apogee

At the outbreak of the Boer War, Queen Victoria's empire was the largest in history, encompassing a quarter of the earth's land mass and embracing 372 million subjects. In the previous decade alone its territorial acquisitions were 50 times larger in size than the mother country itself. Britain itself had but a population of just 40 million people. In sheer geographical terms the scale of overseas possessions was immense: in North America there was Canada, in South America, British Honduras (Belize) and British Guiana (Guyana). In Africa there were vast stretches in every direction: Egypt and, soon, the Sudan in the north, in the west, what is now Guinea, Sierra Leone and Nigeria, in the east, present-day Kenya, and in the south, Cape Colony, Rhodesia (Zimbabwe) and other possessions, later to become South Africa, Zambia, and Botswana. In Asia, there was Hong Kong, Malaya, Singapore, Burma, New Guinea, India, and other territories. In addition to Australia and New Zealand, there were many island possessions in the Pacific, Atlantic and Indian Oceans, and the Mediterranean and Caribbean Seas, amongst these Ceylon, Jamaica, and Cyprus, and Gibraltar.

Imperialism was advantageous to Britain: it satisfied a deep-seated national desire for power and glory. British commercial and martial traditions had been formed over centuries, influenced by geographical, historical and political factors. Extending British power and influence abroad could be legitimized simply on the basis of national and cultural superiority. Imperialism was pursued by many almost as a vocation. Rule over a quarter of the earth's surface was considered not merely a right, but a duty – a duty to bring British ideas, the Christian faith, language, technology, medicine, education, liberal government and, as Victorians saw them, enlightened attitudes.

Justice would prevail, suffering be reduced and ignorance be overcome, all through the introduction (or imposition) of British rule. Arnold Wilson, who trained for a career in the colonial service, described himself and others in his profession as

acolytes of a cult – Pax Britannica – for which we worked happily and, if need be, died gladly. We read our Bibles, many of us, lived full lives, and loved and laughed much, but we knew, as we did so, that though for us all, the wise and the foolish, the slaves and the great, for emperor and for anarchist, there is one end, yet would our work live after us, and by our fruits we should be judged in the days to come.

The power and prestige of the Empire reached its zenith at the time of the Diamond Jubilee of 1897, a time when to the British public the concept of imperialism was morally irreproachable. The notion of imposing one's will, on a national level, on what were universally perceived to be the less civilized peoples of Africa, Asia and the West Indies appeared at the time downright laudable. Ideas which have subsequently been condemned as patronizing, exploitative, racially or culturally superior, or even brutal, remained very much the mainstream view in Victorian Britain. Taking up 'the White Man's burden' signified a duty to civilize, not a license to abuse. According to the Governor of Ceylon, Sir West Ridgeway, in his Jubilee speech,

it dispelled the darkness of ignorance, the scales fell from their eyes, the sordid mists which obscured their view were driven away, and they saw for the first time before them, the bright realm of a glorious Empire.

Even amongst the subject peoples themselves, the time had not yet arrived when nationalism would sow the seeds of discontent and lead growing numbers, particularly in the more advanced colonies like India, to question imperial servitude. Indeed, British dominion seemed to offer to millions of people, ruler and ruled alike, more benefits than shortcomings.

Britons were naturally immensely proud of the fact that the British Empire at the time of Victoria's Jubilee was the largest in history. It is of course no coincidence that the climax of imperial power was attained at the end of a century during which Britain had played a dominant role, very much the position assumed by the United States in the following century. The British had, after all, been the victors at Trafalgar and Waterloo; in banking, trade and manufacturing they were pre-eminent. They were supreme, though not altogether uncontested, at sea. This happy circumstance meant more than mere dominance in the world of commerce, making possible exploration and, above all, colonization. This in turn allowed a massive increase in emigration and the consequent peopling of far-off lands – Canada, South Africa, Australia and New Zealand. Settlers of English-speaking stock swelled the labor force, stimulating the spread of new and exciting forms of technology and hallmarks of European civilization: railways, telegraph lines, underwater telephone cables, hospitals, schools, bridges, roads, and canals.

The British wallowed in self-admiration. These were the people, after all, whose forebears not only beat the French, but drubbed the Russians too, conquered India, suppressed slavery, punished wayward native princes throughout Africa and Asia, and spread their excess capital to every corner of the world in order to finance the infrastructure of modern civilization. Missionaries had converted pagans in large numbers, explorers had located the source of the Nile, discovered previously unknown lakes and regions in the heart of Africa, and brought to light scores of plant and animal species and dinosaur remains of which their Georgian forbears had been entirely

ignorant. The Royal Navy – by far the strongest in the world – seemed to exemplify Britain's invincibility, and her ability to transport her forces to any part of the globe, whether to quell rebellion, conquer new lands or simply make the British presence felt. The soldiers whom the fleet conveyed had shown themselves to be superior to practically every adversary.

The Diamond Jubilee of 1897 offered an opportunity, never repeated again on such a scale, to celebrate this imperial apogee. The spirit of the age was represented that summer by the grandest procession ever seen in London, with the spectacle repeated across the Empire on a smaller scale. The 50,000 troops – thought to be the largest body of soldiers ever assembled in the capital – were drawn from diverse colonies: Malays, Canadians, South Africans, Nigerian tribesmen, Hong Kong police, Cypriots, Maoris, Indian lancers and even head-hunters from North Borneo, not to mention thousands of British troops, all splendidly turned out. National pride soared that day as never before, heightened by patriotic songs and brass bands, the presence of foreign dignitaries and, of course, the Empress-Queen herself.

G. W. Steevens described the scene as 'a pageant which for splendour of appearance and especially for splendour of suggestion has never been paralleled in the history of the world.' A *Times* journalist was even more fulminating:

History may be searched, and searched in vain, to discover so wonderful an exhibition of allegiance and brotherhood amongst so many myriads of men...The mightiest and most beneficial Empire ever known in the annals of mankind.

The whole affair harkened back to the days of Imperial Rome, with tributes brought from throughout the Empire, and long processions of foreign soldiers playing the role of the old barbarian contingents once drawn from the fringes of Gaul, Iberia and Britannia.

London was now the center of imperial power and, to some, effectively the center of the world. The fact that longitude was measured through Greenwich seemed to confirm this. The Jubilee celebrations in this new Rome were meant to publicize to the world in a grand show of pomp and self-congratulation, the greatness of the Empire and Britain's apparently unassailable position in the world. Patriotic sentiment ran at fever pitch. There was as yet no sign of the cracks which were to emerge with the new century. History appeared to favor the growth of the Empire – a trend stretching back to Elizabethan times. One had only to glance at a map of the world to confirm this: Britain's dominions in red stretched across every continent, illustrating the adage: 'the sun never sets on the British Empire.'

The Empire served as an outlet for the pent-up energies of a small, but highly industrialized and dynamic nation on the periphery of the European continent. An abundance of capital existed, ready for investment in construction, commerce and a host of other projects, often on grand scales. The sheer length and breadth of the Empire offered endless opportunities for business, exploration and settlement. Some motives for imperialism were dubious, others transparently selfish, while still others were based on honorable intentions. The wealth, ingenuity, technological sophistication and excitement of Victorian Britain provided the means behind the 'New Imperialism' which, since the 1870s, had captured the imagination of the public in what amounted almost to a craze.

Glory and, perhaps above all, the pursuit of profit, motivated the builders of empire. There was no shortage of opportunity to make money, sometimes on a lavish scale. The ships plying the sea lanes from imperial to British ports bore testimony to the wealth to be made by importing raw materials from across the world. Gold and furs came from Canada, animal skins, diamonds, gold, and wine from southern Africa, silk, rice, tea and precious stones from the Far East, ivory from west and central Africa, cotton from Egypt and India, and food, minerals and other raw materials such as wood, wool, and rubber from various other British possessions. There was nothing, in fact, that the Empire could not provide, either to be consumed at home, or employed in a manufacturing process to create something else for domestic and foreign markets alike. The quest for wealth tempted many to leave Britain's shores forever. It has been shown that gold and diamond discoveries in South Africa attracted thousands of British prospectors to the region. The same occurred, though on a smaller scale, with respect to the gold and silver mines of Australia and the Yukon. If few could attain the wealth of Rhodes, many thousands tried nonetheless.

A far more secure method of pursuing one's millions lay in trade. Though perhaps not as exciting as laying claim to a plot of land and digging for precious minerals, it formed, together with the manufacturing it made possible, the backbone of Britain's economic strength and prowess. Vast quantities of raw materials flowed into Britain, to be processed or otherwise reproduced in some new form for re-export, not least to the developing territories of the Empire: machinery, railway equipment, weapons, carriages, clothing, steel and all manner of luxuries. Profitable markets were ubiquitous, and the era produced more than its fair share of trading barons, merchant princes and capitalists. With the concept of Free Trade in force, the cornucopia of imperial goods found willing consumers, who in turn created a new generation of business tycoons.

Fields for new investment were also legion, and capital was available in prodigious sums. These were put, for better or for worse, in goldfields, plantations, trading companies, railways, insurance companies, and shipping lines. British banks and private investors provided the funding, and with the railway boom over in Britain itself, the Empire offered new and exciting opportunities for profit not only for firms and individual stockholders, but for the nation as a whole. Britain remained, though not for much longer, the richest nation on earth, and much of this may be attributed to the wealth generated by the Empire. At the time of the Jubilee British exports exceeded £216 million annually, compared to £181 million for the United States and £148 million for Germany. British overseas investments amounted to the equivalent of 15 percent of the national capital, which brought in about £100 million a year in interest alone. The nation's gold reserves far exceeded those of any other European country, and the pound remained the strongest and most stable currency in the world.

Capital alone did not account for the enthusiasm with which millions embraced imperialism. A series of larger-than-life characters – men such as Bentham, Tennyson, Disraeli and Cardinal Newman, had, in their own ways and at different periods in the 19th century, promoted various grand designs. The wider world offered space, wealth, and power, Christian redemption, and education for the masses of the 'Dark Continent' and elsewhere. Even science, according to prevailing opinion, stood on their side. Charles Darwin's theories on natural order in the context of the animal kingdom, were applied conveniently, if perhaps dubiously, to the social realm of human relationships, suggesting to many Victorians that as a race they were not merely fit to rule over ignorant 'savages', but possessed a right to do so as natural-born leaders.

Victorians had also undergone a long period of Christian revival, including a strong element of evangelism which could now be diffused throughout an empire containing millions of ignorant 'heathens'. Prominent boarding schools also played their part, with noted reformers such as Dr. Arnold, at Rugby, introducing ideas of public and colonial service as an obligation of the privileged – a form of *noblesse oblige*. The growing international awareness was by no means the exclusive preserve of the upper classes. The 1870 Education Act having introduced compulsory education to all, by 1897 a whole generation had emerged with knowledge of an outside world whose exotic appeal was highlighted in contemporary stories of adventure by authors such as Rudyard Kipling, bringing the excitement of far-off lands into sharp contrast with the dreary realities of Britain's industrial cities. Why stay at home when adventure, if not wealth, beckoned?

The masses need not even to turn to classroom textbooks to discover the virtues of imperialism. The penny press – the forerunners of the modern tabloids – championed the cause of empire-building and found a newly-enfranchised readership hungry for its patriotic, highly intoxicating sentiments, frequently cast in fiercely aggressive tones. If living memory could no longer stretch to the days of Nelson and Wellington, there was no shortage of contemporary imperial heroes to inspire the public. Napier, Wolseley, Kitchener, Cardigan, Havelock, Gordon, Livingstone, and Burton and many others, personified a nation seemingly destined to conquer the 'wicked' and rule with benign paternalism.

External political and economic factors certainly played their part in accelerating and justifying Britain's scramble for, and consolidation of, imperial possessions. The concept of 'Splendid Isolation' appeared to be under threat. The fact that there were rival contenders for new overseas possessions – Germany, France, Italy, and Belgium – only heightened the frenzy. Britain had been the arbiter of Continental affairs since 1815; Germany now vied for the same position, and also for naval supremacy through the rapid expansion of its High Seas Fleet. Germany also had extensive holdings in both southwest and southeast Africa and had extended its interests into the Pacific.

Commercially, Britain's dominant industrial position was being eroded by the vast industrial capacity of the United States, as well as by Germany and, to a lesser extent, France. German technological advances in steel-making and the development of chemicals also gave Britain cause for concern. On the political front, the Russians continued to arouse fears over Indian security, specifically along the North-West frontier, while the French had their own imperial agenda, highlighted by Captain Jean-Baptiste Marchand's claims to the upper Nile during the Fashoda Incident of 1897, which nearly sparked open confrontation.

The search for glory, broadly defined, also played a key role in Britain's desire to plant the Union Jack, however inaccessible the land. Glory need not necessarily take a martial form, though it very often did, and in many instances the simple acquisition of territory, almost for the sake of it, formed a motive for imperialism. Successive governments could always point to just causes: defending the honor of the flag; protecting British nationals abroad; punishing one tyrant or another; suppressing slavery; releasing foreign hostages; securing coaling stations for the Royal Navy; or acquiring territory held by potentially hostile inhabitants adjacent to existing imperial domains.

Chauvinism and pugnacity worked in tandem in the late 19th century. Emboldened by the legacies of Trafalgar and Waterloo, Britons felt invincible. The record of the British Army during the century seemed to bear this opinion out. Notwithstanding the tremendous suffering endured by the troops in the Crimea, the Russians had been thoroughly beaten, to which could be added the eternal glory gained for the undaunted troopers of the Light Brigade. The succession of triumphs followed seemingly uninterrupted: in India, the mutinous sepoys were quashed in 1857–58, followed by the Chinese in 1860 and the Maoris a few years later. Mad King Theodore of Abyssinia was punished for his 'misdeeds' in 1867, the Ashantis, in West Africa, were conquered in 1873 and, after initial catastrophe, the Zulus had been trounced in 1879. The Afghans were put in their place in the same year, the rebellious Egyptians were defeated in 1882, and the Dervishes of the Sudan were next in line for a crushing blow, which Kitchener would deliver in 1898.

Such victories – and there were many more besides – were usually hard-fought. Buoyed up by these successes, however, the public generally offered unqualified support to the government's imperial policies. Indeed, a famous music-hall song, inspired by fears of Russian expansion into the Mediterranean in the 1870s, and still popular at the turn of the century, shows something of the popular faith in Britain's might:

We don't want to fight, but, by Jingo, if we do, We've got the ships, we've got the men, we've got the money too.

Emily Hobhouse

Emily Hobhouse (1860–1926), the daughter of a Cornish rector, championed many humanitarian causes in the course of her life, but she is best remembered, above all in South Africa, for her tireless efforts to bring to the attention of the British public the plight of the tens of thousands of Boer civilians forcibly interned in concentration camps between 1900 and 1902. Alarmed by stories of civilian distress, Hobhouse obtained sponsorship from a relief society and on her own initiative set out to visit some of the camps in the Orange River and Cape Colonies. Horrified by what she saw, she drew up a report of her findings which led to radical improvement in camp conditions and ultimately saved thousands of lives.

The camps were born, the British authorities insisted, out of military and humanitarian necessity. The policy of internment, begun under Roberts after the occupation of Johannesburg and made official under Kitchener in December 1900, had its precedent in the Cuban insurrection of 1896–97, when the notorious Spanish general, Valeriano Weyler, had established camps on the island which resulted in the deaths of about 20,000 internees.

The British camps consisted of rows of canvas tents and little else – with no proper protection from the extremes in temperature. The administrators assigned by the army to cope with this massive undertaking generally had no understanding of the task before them, in particular the acute danger of typhoid in overcrowded, unsanitary conditions. Although some camp commandants made the best of a bad situation, many, either through incompetence, negligence or just plain heartlessness, consigned thousands of civilians, white and black, to a miserable end.

Supported by the Committee of the Distress Fund for South African Women and Children,

Hobhouse, unfairly branded a 'pro-Boer' by dint of her vociferous yet peaceful anti-war campaigning, set out at the end of 1900 with supplies to be distributed among the camps. On arriving in South Africa she received permission to undertake this work from Sir Alfred Milner and Lord Kitchener, and promptly left for Bloemfontein with £200 worth of foodstuffs, and as much clothing as she could take. Unaware of the true extent of the suffering, Hobhouse initially believed she was bringing gifts to those in need rather than in excessive distress. It was not long before the full horror of the camps was revealed. The scale of the suffering was shocking. On 26 January 1901 she reached a camp on the exposed veld at Bloemfontein:

Imagine the heat outside the tents, and the suffocation inside! We sat on their khaki blankets, rolled up, inside Mrs. Botha's tent; and the sun blazed through the single canvas, and flies lay thick and black on everything – no chair, no table, nor any room for such; only a deal box, standing on its end, served as a wee pantry. In this tiny tent live Mrs. Botha, five children (three quite grown up) and a little Kaffir servant girl. Many tents have more occupants ...Wet nights the water streams down through the canvas and comes flowing in (as it knows how to do in this country) under the flap of the tent, and wets their blanket as they lie on the ground.

The numerous occupants, moreover, had to share inadequate rations. A few days later Hobhouse discovered '… a girl of twenty-one lay dying on a stretcher. The father, a big, gentle Boer, kneeling beside her; while, next tent, his wife was watching a child of six, also dying, and one of about five drooping.'

Hobhouse moved on to inspect other camps, including Norval's Pont, Aliwal North, Springfontein, Kimberley and Mafeking.

Boer women and children in a British concentration camp, as portrayed by a French journal, January 1901. In cramped, unhygienic conditions, disease became rife, rapidly spreading amongst the camps' most vulnerable occupants: young children. (Ann Ronan Picture Library)

Almost everywhere she encountered squalid conditions, varying according to the location of the camp, availability of food, water and fuel, the attitude and abilities of the commandant, and a host of other factors. In general, however, she found appalling conditions of overcrowding, woefully inadequate sanitation, poor food, tainted water supplies, and insufficient medical care, not to mention the less critical matters like the absence of beds, furniture and schooling for the children. She returned to Bloemfontein camp on 22 April, only to discover that the population had doubled in size to nearly 4,000 people in the six weeks since her first visit. The Springfontein camp had grown six times from 500 to 3,000 internees, with hundreds more on the way. The authorities were simply unable to cope with the growing numbers.

Hobhouse was particularly moved by the suffering of children, whose rising mortality rates could largely be attributed to disease and malnutrition. In a letter home she described

the death of an infant whose mother had fashioned a makeshift tent out of a strip of canvas in order to shield her sick child. 'The mother,' Hobhouse wrote,

sat on her little trunk, with the child across her knee. She had nothing to give it and the child was sinking fast ... There was nothing to be done and we watched the child draw its last breath in reverent silence.

The mother neither moved nor wept, it was her only child. Dry-eyed but deathly white she sat there motionless looking not at the child but far far away into the depths of grief beyond all tears. A friend stood behind her who called upon Heaven to witness the tragedy, and others crouching on the ground around her wept freely. The scene made an indelible impression on me.

Hobhouse fought hard to draw the attention of the military authorities to the most immediate needs of the internees: better facilities, food, medicines, clothing, soap and every manner of basic amenity and comfort.

Unable to secure these changes, she decided to return home to publicize her findings and exert pressure directly on the Government. She sailed for Britain on 7 May, unaware that the evidence she had gathered in South Africa would prove the catalyst for real change. Already there had been questions in Parliament. In March, two members of Parliament had referred to 'concentration camps' and, bowing reluctantly to pressure, the Government released statistics on the numbers of internees in April and May 1901: 21,000 in the Transvaal camps, 20,000 in the Orange River Colony, and 2,500 in Natal. All told, there were approximately 60,000 interned civilians. No clear figures could be provided for the number of fatalities, nor could officials confirm the number of blacks held in camps of their own. The British policy of racial segregation demanded that Boers and blacks be kept in separate camps.

Hobhouse published her report in June. It contained stark and unexaggerated facts. Her tone was moderate and her recommendations compelling. She had the sense to reserve her bombastic attacks for her private interviews and personal letters. The report stirred the hearts of thousands and attracted the attention of many prominent politicians, who roundly condemned the policies behind scorched earth and the concentration camps, policies described by the anti-war leader of the opposition, Sir Henry Campbell-Bannerman, as 'methods of barbarism'.

Immediately forced on to the defensive, the Government could no longer ignore the issue. Public opinion had been aroused and although the Government continued to insist that the camps served a dual military and humanitarian role – at once denying the guerrillas their sources of support while feeding and housing those whose homes by necessity had been destroyed – it was compelled to institute effective changes to what was increasingly seen as an odious system. In addition, the Government, yielding to Hobhouse's suggestions, appointed Millicent Fawcett to head a women's commission which was to travel to South Africa and report on the state of the camps. Hobhouse was specifically excluded because of the 'sympathy' she had shown to the Boers. Yet, undeterred by this snub, she decided to continue to monitor improvements for herself, and returned to South Africa in October. Kitchener, citing martial law, refused her permission to land, and had 'that bloody woman' forcibly transferred to a troop-ship for deportation.

Her earlier efforts were nevertheless soon vindicated. In December the Fawcett Commission's report confirmed Hobhouse's original findings, recommended the adoption of her suggestions, and added many more besides. As a result, by the end of the war the death rate in the camps had fallen to only 2 percent, though not before thousands had succumbed. Many Afrikaners would carry a legacy of bitterness towards the British well into the new century.

At the end of the war the true, appalling scale of the tragedy could be tabulated: almost 28,000 Boers had died in the 46 concentration camps. Women accounted for two-thirds of the adult deaths. Nearly 80 percent of the fatalities were children under 16 years old, most commonly dying from measles, pneumonia, dysentery and typhoid. Official figures record 14,000 deaths among the 115,000 black Africans interned, but the true figure is now thought to be closer to 20,000. Neither Emily Hobhouse, who ran short of funds, nor Millicent Fawcett, who faced no such obstacle, visited any of the black camps, though Hobhouse at least expressed the view that '... these need looking into badly.' Consequently, the full picture of the plight of Africans interned during the Boer War is not clear. What is clear, however, is that, though the camps did not represent a deliberate policy of genocide, they may rightly be condemned as the product of gross indifference by British government officials remote from the scene, together with culpable negligence on the part of many of the camp administrators actually present.

Emily Hobhouse played a decisive part in exposing the inhumanity of her Government's policy, thereby setting in train a host of reforms that went far in alleviating the suffering of thousands of innocent civilians. Nor did her work cease with the end of the war. In 1902 she published a book on the camps entitled *The Brunt of the War and Where It Fell*, the royalties of which, together with money raised through a 'furnishing fund' she had started in Britain, were used to assist in the recovery of destitute Boer families whose farms had been burnt.

The following year Hobhouse returned to South Africa where, on encountering severe problems connected with repatriation and compensation, she began a campaign which went far in easing the situation. Later, in the interests of reconciliation and rehabilitation, she began a spinning and weaving school in South Africa, and advised on educational matters in schools in Johannesburg and Pretoria. After her death in 1926, her ashes were sent from England to be interred in a women's memorial at Bloemfontein. Smuts himself wrote to Hobhouse's nephew to describe the event: 'It was a great occasion and we buried her like a princess.'

Vereeniging

More than a year before the war actually ended, peace talks had opened at Middelburg between Louis Botha and Lord Kitchener on 28 February 1901. These had come about as a result of the latter's suggestion during a time of stalemate, with neither side, in the event, prepared to give much ground. The negotiations were cordial but there were a number of difficult questions to settle. Initially, both sides brought forward grievances concerning the conduct of their respective opponent. Botha raised the issue of the British arming of natives, while Kitchener, who offered fairly lenient terms, expressed anger over the wearing of British uniforms by some Boer soldiers.

Peace terms naturally dominated the discussions. Boer demands included the prompt return of prisoners; ultimate

Boer soldiers held in the prisoner of war camp at Bloemfontein. Eventually such camps in South Africa proved unable to cope with the number of captives and recourse was made to facilities in St Helena, Ceylon, India, and Bermuda. About 25,000 republican prisoners were in British hands at the end of the war. (Ann Ronan Picture Library)

self-government for the former Boer republics; the use of Dutch and English in schools and courts; Boer debts to be cleared up to £1 million; reconstruction money to be offered; blacks not to be permitted the vote before the colonies were granted self-governing status; and a general amnesty to be extended to all former Boer combatants, including Cape rebels, though the latter were to be disenfranchised.

The Salisbury Government rejected these terms, in particular those relating to amnesty for Cape rebels, and to blacks' rights, which Chamberlain insisted should be the same in the new colonies as those held in the Cape Colony. Botha was not prepared to compromise on the crucial point of the republics' independence. The Middelburg talks therefore failed, though the issues discussed there would ultimately serve as the basis for the successful talks at Vereeniging the following year.

Discussions proposing the establishment of formal peace talks began on 11 April 1902, the same day as the last battle of the war at Roodewal. Kitchener had informed the Boers that the Dutch had offered to mediate, and

though the British Government refused to accept this offer, Kitchener made known the possibility of direct talks to settle a conflict which was now rapidly petering out. A Boer delegation consisting of Botha, Smuts, De Wet and Steyn arrived at Pretoria where they stunned Kitchener by proposing terms strikingly similar to those Kruger had rejected at Bloemfontein three years before. It seemed clear the Boers appreciated that the war was in fact unwinnable. They still insisted, however, on the independence of the republics, ignoring the fact that they had been all but vanquished and occupied. In London, the government swiftly called for unconditional surrender, though one concession, essentially symbolic in nature, was offered: Milner was instructed to take part. This order indicates the tacit recognition that the republics were still sovereign states. As a political rather than a military representative at the talks, his participation suggested that this was more than simply a surrender arranged between opposing commanders, but a political settlement between two nations, despite the fact that, technically, neither the Orange Free State nor the Transvaal actually existed as nation states.

The Boer delegates requested an armistice in order that they could consult with their own representatives abroad as well as with their own commanders still in the field. They, in turn, could gauge the views of their own men. Kitchener refused to allow communication with Boers abroad, but in an unprecedented move offered the Boer delegates unhindered use of British railways and telegraphic services to enable consultation with commandos scattered throughout South Africa. He also arranged for safe passage to Vereeniging, south of Johannesburg, where he offered to host formal peace talks in May; for the period of four days prior to the conference, he gave a pledge that British forces would not attack any commando that was to be consulted.

Kitchener was anxious to finish the war. He had already been offered the post of Commander-in-Chief in India, an appointment he wished to take up as soon as possible, and he was genuinely concerned about the physical and human costs of the ongoing war. He was prepared to make concessions for peace, though not extensive ones, and had shown no compunction about ordering the execution of 51 Cape rebels.

Prior to the talks, De Wet had consulted with all the commandos. The units voted on the thorny issue of retaining or yielding independence. The overwhelming majority voted for independence. British representatives informed Burger, Acting-President of the Transvaal, that they would not grant this. De Wet, who felt morally compelled to honor the views of his compatriots in the field, announced, therefore, his readiness to carry on the fight. Jan Smuts and Barry Hertzog (1866–1942) now intervened, bringing their legal knowledge to bear on the issue. They averted deadlock, successfully arguing that delegates were not in fact compelled to follow the views of the commandos, but must regard them merely as points for their guidance. They were free, as representatives of the burghers at large, to proceed in the best interests of their people.

Five negotiators were formally appointed from among the 60 Boer delegates assembled at Vereeniging who had been elected by the various commandos. These were: Louis Botha, Koos de la Rey and Jan Smuts on behalf of the Transvaal, and Barry Hertzog and Christiaan de Wet for the Orange Free State. In general, those from the Transvaal backed peace, while those from the Free State largely supported continued resistance. President Steyn of the Free State, a staunch 'bitter-ender', was effectively impotent at the peace talks because of ill health. Had he been able to participate fully, he would have been a strong advocate for the continuation of hostilities.

When negotiations began, the Boers offered the Rand, other territories, and control of foreign affairs to Britain in return for self-government in all other matters to be permitted without restriction. Britain was in a strong position and refused. Kitchener had been instructed to follow the Middelburg terms closely, conceding little more than an amnesty for the Cape rebels: independence for the Boer republics was simply not an option. Milner was prepared to cease all discussions but Kitchener was more conciliatory, and in separate informal discussions with Smuts informed him that he predicted a change of government in London within two years. A Liberal government, he suggested, might be prepared to modify the less palatable aspects of any treaty to be signed at Vereeniging. The impasse gradually eased, and the British team drew up a statement calling on the Boers to disarm and accept British sovereignty. If this were signed, other terms would be appended and a formal treaty concluded.

Eventually, Smuts and Hertzog hammered out a draft agreement with Milner and his team, an agreement which bore a striking resemblance to the Middelburg terms. Milner and Kitchener declined to set a deadline for the establishment of South African self-government, but the Boers successfully negotiated concessions over and above the original basis for settlement. Britain, for instance, pledged to pay Boer war debts up to £3 million – triple the amount originally offered. Loans to assist in the rebuilding of houses and farms were to be offered to Boers and loyalists. All adult males were to be eligible to vote, apart from the leaders of the Cape rebels, who would now face a five-year rather than a life exclusion from enfranchisement. Only the leaders of the Cape rebels would now face imprisonment. On the issue of blacks' political rights, the Boers insisted that they were not to be enfranchised until after the colonies became self-governing.

Milner had opposed the peace process all along, for he believed that within a matter of months Britain's military position would permit her to establish her own terms, with himself at the head of the civilian administration of a greater South Africa. Yet his efforts to stall for time failed, and the terms in general were considered very favorable by the Cabinet in London. Nonetheless, ministers expressed doubts on the issues of loans and on native rights. London had no objection to the amount proposed, but the figure offered was to include the repayment of war debts as well.

The issue of native rights proved of far greater concern. It was perfectly clear that if

suffrage were not extended to blacks before British control ceased in South Africa, the Boers, once authority passed into their hands, would simply refuse it. The British Government found this unacceptable. Chamberlain himself had stated before the peace talks: 'We cannot consent to purchase a shameful peace by leaving the Coloured population in the position in which they stood before the war.' Nevertheless, insistence on this point threatened the whole peace process. Milner informed the cabinet that the Boers refused to sign any agreement containing such concessions, adding that: '… there is much to be said for leaving [the] question of political rights of [the] natives to be settled by [the] colonists themselves.' The British Government therefore yielded, leaving the political fate of natives in the hands of a future Afrikaner government. The sacrifice of this issue was to have major implications for the future of race relations in South Africa.

The revised draft treaty arrived back in Pretoria on 27 May and required a simple acceptance or refusal on the part of the Boer leaders by 31 May. Louis Botha led the peace faction within the Boer delegation and justified his position on numerous grounds. Severe shortages of horses and food continued to impede the ability of commandos to operate successfully. Those women and children still on the veld or accompanying the commandos were still suffering extreme hardships. The camps, which had never provided adequate shelter, were now full. Conditions inside were well known to the outside world. Circumstances that led families to wander without shelter and adequate food could, he argued, no longer be tolerated. The blockhouses were gradually immobilizing the remaining commandos, no rebellion was likely to occur in the Cape, and foreign assistance had not materialized.

Yet an even greater concern troubled Botha: the threat, real or imagined, of native attacks on Boer individuals and settlements, many of which, their men still on commando, were effectively defenseless. An incident at Holkrantz, north of Vryheid, which occurred 10 days before the opening of negotiations, underlined this perceived threat. There a commando had raided a Zulu kraal, driving off women and children, stealing the cattle and leaving the settlement in flames. After the local chief, Sikhobobo, protested, the commando leader justified the attacks on the grounds that the Zulus had aided the British. When, in a public statement, he likened the chief and his men to lice, Sikhobobo launched an attack, retaking a large proportion of the cattle originally seized by the Boers and inflicting heavy casualties on the commando concerned. Although no Boer women or children were harmed in the incident, which was the result of direct provocation, some delegates concluded that only peace could give Boer civilians real protection. Botha nevertheless had his critics, particularly delegates from the Free State like De Wet and Steyn who continued to refuse peace without the guarantee of independence. The Free State delegates' position was understandable: they had not had to bear the full impact of the war in the way that the Transvaalers had. Indeed, Steyn was so incensed by the terms that he immediately resigned his presidency. De Wet was left the remaining die-hard against surrender, a true 'bitter-ender.'

The ultimate question now fell to the three senior commanders whose importance in the conflict gave them an implicit authority over the opinions of the other delegates. These were Botha, who advocated peace, De Wet, who favored continuing the war until the republics were granted independence, and Koos de la Rey, who at first remained undecided. Finally, De la Rey concluded that peace, at a time when there were still concessions to be wrung from the settlement, offered the Boers the chance to retain essential elements of their Afrikaner society, such as the education, taxation and legal systems. Further resistance, he maintained, offered more burghers the opportunity to change sides, joining the 5,000 men, including Christiaan de Wet's brother, Piet, who had already offered their services to the British. Peace concluded now, on reasonably favorable terms, offered the opportunity for future independence as a unified Afrikaner nation.

Events took a decisive turn on the morning of 31 May, the day scheduled for the crucial vote. Botha and De la Rey met privately with De Wet in his tent and pleaded for his support. Winning the war was impossible, they argued, and little time remained for an honorable peace. De Wet was ultimately persuaded and the Boer delegates were presented with a document containing six reasons why the British terms ought to be accepted. The policy of scorched earth had rendered further resistance impossible; the concentration camps had already caused untold suffering to Boer civilians; native Africans had openly begun to oppose the Boers, as seen at Holkrantz; the British had issued proclamations threatening the confiscation of Boer land; the Boers possessed no facilities for holding British prisoners; and, finally, there was no realistic chance of victory in the field. When the vote was taken that afternoon, 54 delegates out of 60 supported the treaty terms. The Boer leaders quickly returned to Pretoria and signed the treaty. 'We are good friends again now,' Kitchener said to the Boers as he shook hands with them. Thus was ended, on gentlemanly terms, a conflict that had seen many less civil exchanges between Briton and Boer.

The leaders now had to inform the various units in the field. There were still 21,000 men under arms, though one-fifth of all the Boers engaged in the fighting were now on the British side. Disarmament occurred peacefully, though many were not reconciled to peace. Deneys Reitz recorded the dejection of the beaten troops:

… our men fired away their ammunition into the air, smashed their rifle butts and sullenly flung their broken weapons down, before putting their names to the undertaking which each man was called upon to sign, that he would abide by the peace terms. When my father's turn came, he handed over his rifle, but refused to sign …

Reitz and his father were then forced into exile, paying a high price for their loyalty to a lost cause.

Cost, lessons and legacy

The human cost of the war was high. There were approximately 100,000 British and Imperial casualties, including 22,000 dead. About 6,000 were killed in action, while the remaining 16,000 perished as a result of wounds or disease. In a war many had expected to be 'over by Christmas' but which actually lasted nearly three years, Britain and her empire eventually sent 450,000 men to fight. The Boers lost at least 7,000 of approximately 88,000 who served in the field (which included 2,100 foreign volunteers and 13,000 rebels from the Cape and Natal), in addition to about 28,000

British colonial troops burning a Boer farm. One Australian recounted how 'we burnt hundreds of homes…and had to turn the women & children out in the wet with only a few clothes & very little food. It is a job that I can't stand…We came over to fight men, not women and children.' (Ann Ronan Picture Library)

civilian deaths – mostly women and children who succumbed to disease in the concentration camps. The war cost Britain over £200 million. Of the half a million horses brought to the theater, 335,000 fell, not to mention scores of mules and donkeys.

The war left in its wake a ruined economy and a devastated landscape. The wholesale and widespread destruction of Boer farms, livestock and crops was a new and horrifying feature of the first major conflict of the 20th century. It is impossible to calculate the extent of the damage exactly, but approximately 30,000 homesteads were burned and several million cattle, horses and sheep were either destroyed or carried off. As many as 63,000 Boer families made claims for compensation. Farm-burning had achieved its objective of denying sustenance to the guerrillas, but it left no means of support for families returning from internment. Nor were claims restricted to whites; blacks, who for the most part owned cheaper property and earned far less than their white counterparts, sought a total of £661,000 in compensation for damage inflicted on their homes and livelihoods.

Official contemporary estimates of black African losses, about 7,000, fall far short of the reality. Modern calculations estimate that 115,000 blacks were held in the camps, 20,000 of whom died. To these must be added those unrecorded cases of blacks suspected of working for the British, either as soldiers, scouts, spies or in other capacities, and summarily shot by the Boers. Between 10,000 and 30,000 black Africans were armed by the British Army. Whatever the true figures, they render the traditional view of the conflict as a 'white man's war' wholly insupportable. Blacks played a significant role in the British war effort.

Botha receiving intelligence from black scouts. Both sides employed friendly blacks, usually in non-combatant roles. Those who served the Boers performed heavy labor such as digging trenches. They also drove wagons, scouted and served as *agterryers* or batmen. (Ann Ronan Picture Library)

Milner had hoped that British rule in South Africa would shift the balance of power between Afrikaners and those of British descent. Defeat of the Boer republics ought, he believed, to have dampened the flow of Afrikaner nationalism. He looked for a heavy influx of British immigrants after the war who would gradually transform the existing culture, language and legal structure. With the mines already back in operation and with the reconstruction of the infrastructure underway, industry would once again flourish. Yet the government in London constrained Milner's plans, and predictions of mass immigration proved wildly overoptimistic.

The settlement at Vereeniging confirmed British supremacy in South Africa. Reconstruction was now the urgent task of Lord Alfred Milner, in his expanded role as High Commissioner for South Africa and Governor of the Orange River Colony and the Transvaal. His was a massive undertaking, but assistance was at hand in the form of what became known as 'Milner's

kindergarten,' a group of young, mostly Oxford-educated men such as Lionel Curtis, Patrick Duncan and Richard Feetham. Milner remained in South Africa until 1905, during which time he improved standards of education and expanded communications and railways. He introduced reforms on the pass laws for blacks and improved working conditions in the mines, but most of his reforms catered to whites.

Although the emotional scars of the conflict would prove harder to heal, practical measures to restore normality were swiftly set in motion. Boer prisoners were repatriated quickly from Bermuda, Ceylon and St Helena. Displaced Boer families – in concentration camps, settled in the Cape or wandering the veld – had to be resettled in areas that had been devastated by the systematic policy of farm-burning, as had blacks, 'bitter-enders', 'joiners' and Uitlanders. To deal with the delicate issue of 'joiners', separate repatriation councils were established.

Even the process of returning internees to their farmsteads took time. They could not simply leave on foot. Many remained in the camps for months after the peace until transport was available for them. Many, of course, never made it out, and Boer men arriving at the camps in search of their families sometimes found that they had lost everything. Marie Proudfoot described this all too frequent scene:

You know there are people who, when they arrived at the camps, everybody in their families were dead. There was nobody – no child, no wife, nobody. They signed the peace, nobody was left ... The man would stand there with his hat on his head and his horse at his arm ... he would look for them. 'Where are they?' And somebody would say, 'Over there in the cemetery.' Those poor women.

Economic recovery proceeded apace with the influx of British loans. Vereeniging provided £3 million, together with nearly the same amount in interest-free loans for Boer resettlement and to provide food, medicine, and shelter for immediate need in areas hardest hit by the war. In addition, £2 million was available for Uitlanders, blacks and neutral foreigners. Priority was given to the rebuilding of farms. Tools and seeds were provided to landowners. Total repatriation and resettlement costs ran to approximately £16.5 million.

Reconstruction also served to regenerate the economy as a whole, particularly the mining industry, and Milner had begun this work before the war was over, together with his 'kindergarten.' Significant progress was made in returning to and exceeding prewar levels of gold production, so that, whereas in 1903 production stood at £12.6 million, it increased to £27.5 million in 1907, an increase which went far in preparing the region for union only a few years later. This was partly achieved by Milner's controversial policy of importing indentured Chinese laborers, a move strongly criticized by the new Liberal government in London when it was discovered that they were being flogged, and by Afrikaners, who banded together in opposition to these newcomers, backed, ironically, by Uitlanders who saw their own wages threatened by the willingness of the Chinese to work down the mines at very low wages. It was also achieved by strict adherence to the pass laws and tough controls imposed on the cost of native labor.

For ordinary Boers, the hardship caused by the destruction of their homes and farms was greatly exacerbated by a series of droughts in 1902 and again in 1903. The numbers of whites in the Orange Free State living in poverty had been quite low before the war, in spite of an increase in the Transvaal. After the war, however, there were sharp rises in white poverty in both former republics, with landowners so destitute that they had not even the means of accommodating the landless. Those who had been 'joiners' or 'hands-uppers' were particularly hard hit.

Some of the landless and collaborators were rehoused in newly established settlements in the eastern and western Transvaal, but many formerly rural whites, left with nothing, made for the cities in large numbers, desperate to find work in industry and mining. Society consequently underwent some dramatic and not always desirable changes. Traditional rural life began to disappear with the growth of the urban base and the new prosperity brought by the influx of capital, mostly from Britain. A new generation of Afrikaners now found they had money in their pockets, and began to harbor political ambitions.

Black South Africans suffered the greatest hardship as a result of the war. Resettlement of those blacks formerly accommodated in camps did take place, but proper recovery was hindered by the lack of farm tools and seed, largely due to the disproportionate assistance provided to whites. The Native Refugee Department in the Transvaal, for instance, received just over £16,000 compared to the nearly £1.2 million provided to the Repatriation Department for white resettlement and the rebuilding of farms. In several parts of the Transvaal, where the devastation had been particularly acute, thousands of blacks continued to suffer from near-starvation even six months after the end of hostilities. With successive droughts worsening an already dreadful situation, many blacks had no choice but to become wage-earners working for white farmers where, before, they were landowners in their own right. For blacks who had formerly been employed in the mines, there were no improvements in working conditions. Indeed, wages fell, controls over workers increased and conditions declined.

Those tribes which had served the victors had good reason for disillusionment after the war. The Kgatla, who had prevented the Boers from operating on their lands, had hoped for an amalgamation of their reserve in the western Transvaal with the remainder of the tribe in the Bechuanaland Protectorate. This never occurred. The Pedi hoped for additional land in return for loyalty to the British cause, but this was not forthcoming either. And the Zulus found much of their land opened to white settlement. Segale, a chief of the Bakgatla, wrote in 1903 that, 'I truly believe that if there is a war again the people of the Transvaal will assist the Boers ... The natives of the Transvaal say, 'we expected deliverance whereas we have gone deeper into bonds.''

Blacks also lost on the political front, for British victory did not bring the hoped-for political reforms necessary for the extension to the new colonies of the franchise already in force in the Cape. Not only were there no black representatives at the talks, their rights were not even represented. Vereeniging only postponed the resolution of the question of political rights for blacks, coloreds and Indians until the new colonies achieved self-governing status. Milner's administration did nothing to reverse this, and the treaty did not require the Boers to effect change. Laws in the Transvaal and Free State which discriminated against blacks not only remained in force, but in some cases extended into new areas of life. All of this was tacitly sanctioned by the Treaty of Vereeniging, which effectively retained the status quo of white supremacy in South Africa. There was no reason to suppose self-governing Afrikaner states would freely extend the franchise to the black majority. Salisbury's words of February 1900, it seemed, now amounted to nothing:

There must be no doubt ... that due precaution will be taken for the kindly and improving treatment of those countless indigenous races of whose destiny I fear we have been too forgetful.

The rights of the blacks had been overlooked once again.

For white South Africans the war had a number of effects on society and politics. Milner's policy of Anglicizing the region both in terms of language and culture, and of discouraging Afrikaner nationalism, had failed utterly. Since the massive British immigration he had hoped for had not materialized, he had no desire for the new colonies to form any self-governing federation to include Cape Colony and Natal. Some Boers became permanent outcasts as a result of collaboration, but by embracing a policy of reconciliation Louis Botha made considerable strides in reshaping Afrikaner society, strengthened by general perceptions of the inadequacy of British compensation held by everyone from 'bitter-enders' to 'joiners' and resentment of Milner's policy of Anglicization. General calls for forgiveness reached sympathetic ears for the most part.

This process was helped by the fact that the Boers could focus outwards on the British as the cause of their travails.

A war fought on South African soil, involving the citizens of the two republics, necessarily had a profound impact on Afrikaner identity. The Boer people had fought for the ideal of independence, they had produced great leaders, they had defied one of the greatest powers on earth, and they had suffered greatly in what some held to be a divine cause. This new sense of pride led to a cultural revival that established and promoted Afrikaans as a fundamental part of the region's identity.

Political revival went hand in hand with cultural revival. In the aftermath of war several political parties sprang to life, such as the Het Volk Party under Botha, Burger, Koos de la Rey and Smuts, established in 1905 in the Transvaal. In the former Free State men such as Barry Hertzog, Abraham Fischer and Christiaan de Wet founded the Orangia Unie in 1906. Milner's hopes of an end to Afrikaner nationalism were dashed within a few years of war's end.

In Britain the Liberal Party won the election of 1905, and Henry Campbell-Bannerman became Prime Minister. The implications for South Africa were significant in two ways: first, Milner was recalled, though his subordinates remained behind in the administration. Second, Campbell-Bannerman's government granted self-rule to the Transvaal in December 1906, followed by the same concession to the Orange River Colony the following June. Louis Botha was elected Prime Minister of the Transvaal in the general elections of 1907, while in the Orange River Colony Abraham Fischer became Prime Minister.

The Progressive Party, headed by Jameson, won the Cape elections of 1904, but three years later, by which time all four British South African colonies shared similar political systems, interest both within British loyalist and Afrikaner circles turned towards unification. Afrikaner political ascendancy was achieved when in the following year the South African party, led by John Merriman, won the general election in the Cape, leaving Natal as the only British colony in South Africa which was not under Afrikaner leadership. It was now only a matter of time before nationalists held sway over imperialists, and the Union of South Africa came into being on 31 May 1910 as a self-governing dominion of the British Empire, with Louis Botha the first Prime Minister. The war denied the Boers their independence, but the loss was very temporary.

Reconciliation with Britain, rapid reconstruction and finally, independence, provided the conditions necessary for South Africa to participate on Britain's side in the First World War. South African troops played a major role in operations against Germany's African colonies. There was, nevertheless, some resistance, which took the form of a short-lived rising led by Christiaan de Wet and Kemp. This was suppressed but resulted in the accidental death of De la Rey. In the Second World War South African troops took a prominent role, particularly in the North African campaigns.

Blacks in South Africa were left to face a long and trying period of subjugation. Britain's failure to secure enfranchisement for them in

Picket of the 13th Hussars surprised near the Tugela River. British patrols were regularly harassed by Boer commandos, who possessed a superior knowledge of the country. (Ann Ronan Picture Library)

the peace settlement confirmed the fears of many who insisted that the Boers would never grant them equality. To be sure, quite apart from British actions, the war itself solidified Boer attitudes about racial inequality and oppression – a reality which would characterize South African politics until the end of the 20th century. The roots of apartheid lay much deeper than Vereeniging, but the basis for white rule after the establishment of the Republic of South Africa may in part be attributed to the failure of British peacemakers at the end of the Boer War to guarantee black political rights in the former Boer republics. Article 8 of the treaty effectively relegated blacks to nearly a century of white minority rule. When the issue arose again in 1909 during discussions concerning the establishment of the Union, Britain made no objection to the continued black disenfranchisement, thereby putting paid to any claims that the cause of racial equality played more than a subordinate role in Britain's war aims. Vereeniging was not, then, directly responsible for the establishment of apartheid after the National Party under Daniel Malan took power in 1948, but it is clear that a vital opportunity to establish political equality was lost at the moment of victory.

Perhaps the greatest paradox of the war was the fact that, though Britain emerged the

victor in the military sense, the Boers clearly won the peace. Within a decade of the end of hostilities all four South African Crown colonies had been unified into a self-governing union dominated by Afrikaners. The Boer republics had gone to war in the name of liberty and now they had achieved it. Natal and the Cape Colony had been subsumed in the process. The Boers were now free to shape their society as they wished. A completely independent Republic of South Africa came into being in 1961, on the 59th anniversary of the Treaty of Vereeniging.

The war had important implications for the future of the British Army, not least because there clearly had to be lessons to be gleaned from a conflict that had dealt such a profound blow to the military and moral prestige of the Empire. The war had largely been fought in open, undulating country, with the attacker often exposed to accurate, repeating rifle fire directed by men concealed by their use of smokeless powder and slit trenches. These were clear precursors of First World War methods. Paradoxically, topography dictated that success depended heavily on the side exercising superior mobility. Thus, the horse – that same instrument of war that all great armies since ancient times had employed – retained paramount importance. Such contradictory features of the war made the task of preparing for the next conflict all the more difficult.

Virtually every regiment in the army had served in South Africa and the public's keen interest in the course of the conflict and in the condition of the army, led particularly by Lord Roberts, ensured the introduction of numerous reforms in the coming decade. The Elgin Commission, established in 1903, studied the lessons of the conflict and took statements from numerous officers on the conduct of the war and the state of the troops. Reforms were introduced the following year, after the Esher Committee published its conclusions.

The office of Commander-in-Chief was abolished, its place taken by the Army Council which was in turn, through the Secretary of State for War, accountable to the cabinet on all military matters. The Esher Committee's findings also led to the establishment of the

Committee of Imperial Defence, which provided advice on coordinating policy between the major relevant Government departments and the armed forces across the empire. In 1907, the Secretary of State for War, Haldane, created a general staff, and the various voluntary units were replaced by the Territorial Army, with the specific task of home defense. Numerous other reforms, some of which met with criticism and downright opposition, were introduced in this period, greatly improving the training and organization of the army.

When, in August 1914, Britain went to war against Germany, the British Expeditionary Force (BEF), consisting of four divisions, could be deployed in France remarkably quickly, where it acquitted itself well against superior numbers. Whereas the divisions deployed in South Africa had had no peacetime experience training together, those of the BEF benefited from pre-war joint exercises. At least one lesson of the Boer War could not be applied to the new demands of warfare in 1914: whereas mounted troops had been shown to be indispensable on the open plains of South Africa, they were utterly useless on the Western Front in 1914. Appalling losses were suffered in the face of trenches, barbed wire and machine guns.

Moreover, the dominant role played by the cavalry in South Africa had lent added prestige to this arm, with the result that many of the principal commanders in the First World War were drawn from the highest ranks of that romantic, but now virtually useless, arm. Both British Commanders-in-Chief, Field Marshal Sir John French and Field Marshal Sir Douglas Haig, were cavalry commanders, each of whom not only possessed outmoded ideas on the place of the mounted arm, but failed to understand the proper role of infantry and artillery, both of which had replaced the cavalry as the primary elements of continental European warfare more than a generation before 1914. Nevertheless, the experience gained, the bitter lessons learned, and the reforms undertaken as a result of the Boer War, established the British Army of 1914 as one of the finest fighting forces in the world, and probably the best ever to leave British shores.

Glossary

Afrikaner – a white African/European settler of southern Africa

Boer – farmer

drift – ford; river crossing

commando – the basic Boer military unit

kop/kopje – rocky hill, often steep (latter pronounced 'koppie')

kraal – native village consisting of huts, generally surrounded by a fence

laager – encampment organized for the protection of people and animals

nek – pass

Uitlander – 'outsiders,' the term used by the Boers to describe foreigners

veld – (sometimes spelled 'veldt') open grassland with low-growing scrub and thorny shrubs

Further reading

Literature on the Boer War, both primary and secondary, is vast. Here follows some of the more accessible and useful sources.

Primary sources

Churchill, Winston, *London to Ladysmith via Pretoria*, London, Longmans Green, 1900.

De Wet, Christiaan, *Three Years' War*, London, Constable, 1902.

De la Rey, Jacoba, trans. Lucy Hotz, *A Woman's Wanderings and Trials During the Anglo-Boer War*, London, T. Fisher Unwin, 1903.

Fuller, J. F. C., *The Last of the Gentlemen's Wars: A Subaltern's Journal of the War in South Africa, 1899–1902*, London, Faber & Faber, 1937.

Nevinson, H. W., *Ladysmith: Diary of a Siege*, London, Methuen, 1900.

Pienaar, P., *With Steyn and De Wet*, London, Methuen, 1902.

Plaatje, S. T., *The Boer War Diary of Sol T. Plaatje: An African at Mafeking*, (ed.) J. L. Comaroff, Johannesburg, Macmillan, 1973.

Reitz, Deneys, *Commando: A Boer Journal of the Boer War*, London, Faber & Faber, 1929.

Schikkeerling, R. W., *Commando Courageous*, Johannesburg, Keartland, 1964.

Smuts, Jan, *Memoirs of the Boer War*, (eds) S. B. Spies and Gail Nattrass, Johannesburg, Jonathan Ball, 1966.

Todd, Pamela and Fordham, David, comp., *Private Tucker's Diary*, London, Elm Tree Books, 1980.

Treeves, Frederick, *The Tale of a Field Hospital*, London, Cassell, 1900.

Van Reenen, Rykie, *Emily Hobhouse: Boer War Letters*, Cape Town, Human & Rousseau, 1984.

Secondary sources

Amery, Leo (ed.), *The Times' History of the War in South Africa, 1899–1902* (7 vols), London, Sampson Low, Marston, 1900–1909.

Barthorp, Michael, *The Anglo-Boer Wars*, Poole, Blandford Press, 1987.

Carver, Michael, *The National Army Museum Book of the Boer War*, London, Sidgwick & Jackson, 1999.

Croetzer, Owen, *The Anglo-Boer War: The Road to Infamy*, Rivonia, William Waterman, 1996.

Farwell, Byron, *The Great Boer War*, London, Penguin Books, 1976.

Fisher, John, *Paul Kruger: His Life and Times*, London, Secker & Warburg, 1974.

Gardner, Brian, *Mafeking: A Victorian Legend*, London, Cassell, 1966.

Gooch, John (ed.), *Boer War: Direction, Experience and Image*, London, Frank Cass, 2000.

Hall, Darrell, and (eds) Fransjohan Pretorius and Gilbert Torlage, *The Hall Handbook of the Anglo-Boer War*, Pietermaritzburg, University of Natal Press, 1999.

Hobhouse, Emily, *The Brunt of the War and Where It Fell*, London, Methuen, 1902.

Ingham, Kenneth, *Jan Christiaan Smuts*, London, Weidenfeld & Nicolson, 1986.

Jackson, Tabitha, *The Boer War*, London, Macmillan, 1999.

Judd, Denis and Surridge, Keith, *The Boer War*, London, John Murray, 2002.

Knight, Ian, *Colenso 1899*, Oxford, Osprey Publishing, 1995.

Knight, Ian and Embleton, Gerry, *Boer Wars (2) 1898–1902*, Oxford, Osprey Publishing, 1997.

Kruger, Rayne, *Good-bye Dolly Gray: The Story of the Boer War*, London, Cassell, 1959.

Marix Evans, Martin, *The Boer War: South Africa, 1899–1902*, Oxford, Osprey Publishing, 1999.

Maurice, F. M. and Grant, M. H. (eds), *History of the War in South Africa, 1899–1902* (4 vols), London, Hurst and Blackett, 1906–10. [The UK Official History].

Miller, Stephen M., *Lord Methuen and the British Army: Failure and Redemption in South Africa*, London, Frank Cass, 1999.

Nasson, Bill, *Abraham Esau's War: A Black South African in the Cape, 1899–1902*, Cambridge, Cambridge University Press, 1991.

Nasson, Bill, *The South African War, 1899–1902*, London, Arnold, 1999.

Pakenham, Thomas, *The Boer War*, London Weidenfeld & Nicolson, 1979.

Pemberton, W. Baring, *Battles of the Boer War*, London, Batsford, 1964.

Powell, Geoffrey, *Buller: A Scapegoat? A Life of General Sir Redvers Buller, 1839–1908*, London, Leo Cooper, 1994.

Pretorius, Fransjohan, *The Anglo-Boer War, 1899–1902*, Cape Town, Don Nelson, 1985.

Pretorius, Fransjohan, *Life on Commando During the Anglo-Boer War, 1899–1902*, Cape Town, Human & Rousseau, 1999.

Smith, Iain R. *The Origins of the South African War, 1899–1902*, London, Longman, 1996.

Smurthwaite, David, *The Boer War, 1899–1902*, London, Octopus, 1999.

Spies, S. B., *Methods of Barbarism? Roberts and Kitchener and Civilians in the Boer Republics, January 1900–May 1902*, Cape Town, Human & Rousseau, 1977.

Trew, Peter, *The Boer War Generals*, Stroud, Sutton Publishing, 1999.

Warwick, Peter (ed.), *The South African War: The Anglo-Boer War, 1899–1902*, Harlow, Essex, Longman, 1980.

Warwick, Peter, *Black People and the South African War, 1899–1902*, Cambridge, Cambridge University Press, 1983.

Index

Figures in **bold** refer to illustrations.

Visit the Osprey website

- Information about forthcoming books

- Author information

- Read extracts and see sample pages

- Sign up for our free newsletters

- Competitions and prizes